Amc

©The Secret Jewel ... Cyclades

A Visitor's and Walker's Guide

Paul and Henrietta Delahunt-Rimmer

Published by
Travelleur Publishing
Denby Dale, UK

First published in 2010 by
Travelleur
96 Thorpes Avenue
Denby Dale
Huddersfield HD8 8TB
UK

ISBN 978-0-9556288-2-5

Printed and bound by the Gutenberg Press, Malta

Authors' disclaimer
The authors hold no responsibility for death or injury of any person taking
part in walks described in this book. It is stressed that the text is a 'guide'
not an 'order'!

Jacket photograph courtesy of Peter Hughes.

Contents

Part 1 - General Information

Part 2 - Walks

Appendix

Boules outside Nikos' taverna

Midsummer sunset Agii Anargiri

About The Authors

Paul and Henrietta Delahunt-Rimmer are the founders of 'Nature Trail Amorgos' which was established in 1999. This diversified into Special Interest Holidays, of which they are directors, in 2001. They are both retired Royal Air Force officers. Paul completed 16 years of military service retiring as a senior officer and then went on to be an airline pilot. Henri spent 8 years in the Royal Air Force initially as a nursing sister and then made the unprecedented step of becoming an Air Traffic Control Officer. Henri is also an historian. In the Royal Air Force Paul organised and implemented Royal and Ministerial flights. The extremely high standards required for these operations are reflected in the execution of the business on Amorgos. 1999 was a time for a life-style change. The story of this change, recounted in their book 'Out of the Rat Race into the Fire' is in the making. Although they were familiar with Amorgos they researched many other Greek islands to set up on as the ideal place for Nature lovers and walkers. Amorgos won hands down. Ever since the inception, over 50% of their clients have contacted the company to thank them for their holiday.

Special Interest Holidays is dedicated to Eco-Tourism[1] . Using his business qualifications Paul is a consultant in the matter to the Eco Club, the local council and is working with Elliniki Etairia who are committed to the preservation of nature in Greece. He has written academic papers on the subject and has been asked by the EU for his opinion on eco-tourism in Greece. Practicing what they preach they live up in the mountains, with no road, mains electricity, water, sewage or gas. The local people think that they are slightly deranged but are impressed by their dedication.

In 2009 Special Interest Holidays diversified into luxury safari holidays in Southern Africa[2] .

Only by meeting these people, their staff or reading this guide can you get to know about the real Amorgos and its secret places.

---

[1] See appendix
[2] See appendix: Useful web sites

Island Hospitality

It is indicative of the caring nature of the island people of Amorgos the way they reacted to the first tourists. Nikolaos' grandmother saw tourists in Langada, a very rare sight in those days, grabbed them by the arm and steered them into her house. Her hospitality was incredibly generous. They were given cold meats, salad, cheese, bread, fruit, cakes and retsina. They didn't of course understand Greek neither did they really understand what was going on but the lady was so charming and insistent they felt that she would be insulted if they turned down her generosity. They were in fact absolutely correct and it still applies today. When she was asked by her grandson why she took these people in and fed and watered them she said, 'they were not from the island and they had no family to feed and look after them'. If they had asked her if she knew if there was anywhere they could stay the night there is no doubt that she would have accommodated them. And, would have refused a single drachma in return. In more recent times a friend of ours and his girl friend mistook a private house for a cafeneion. This is very easy to do as some of these establishments are literally the family front room. They walked in through the open front door, made themselves comfortable and ordered drinks. They were a little disappointed at the choice of beverages but settled for glasses of wine which were gladly served to them with great kindness. It is only when they came to pay that they realised their mistake. There was no question of reimbursement of course, indeed the owner appeared insulted by the very suggestion. They left with a little bag of cake and fruit which was foisted upon them to see them through the afternoon. Most visitors to Amorgos find this friendly and generous approach alien to them in the 21st century and wish to reciprocate. It is not expected and money is out of the question. However, the secret is to send some photographs of the hosts and their family back to them, they just love these, and their houses are full of such souvenirs.

Out of the Rat Race into the fire

A taverna kitten

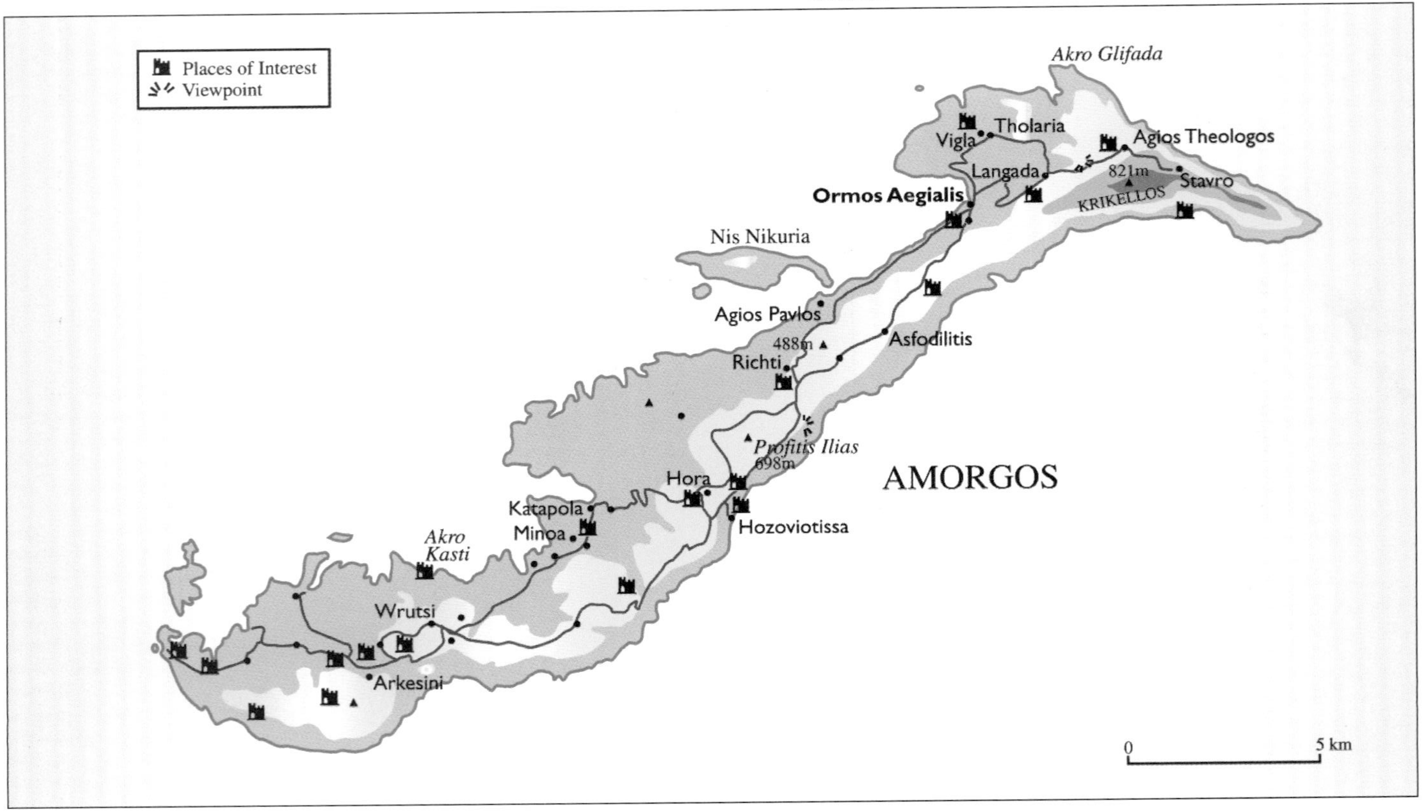

Places of Interest
Viewpoint

5 km

0

Akro Glifada

Agios Theologos
Stavro
821m
KRIKELLOS
Tholaria
Vigla
Langada
Ormos Aegialis
Asfodilitis

AMORGOS

Nis Nikuria

Agios Pavlos
488m
Richti
Profitis Ilias
698m
Hozoviotissa

Hora

Katapola
Minoa

Akro
Kasti

Wrutsi

Arkesini

Acknowledgements

The knowledge gained to write this guide has been the result of fifteen years of research and the extraction of local knowledge by intelligence gathering or corruption and bribery as required. We have been advised by academics in many subjects and assisted by islanders in finding many of the 'hidden places'. We have been forced to spend many hours in local cafeneions and tavernas listening to the stories of old and then try to sift out the truth from some of the outrageous tales. In essence this book is the culmination of many hundreds of minds and memories. We can only single out a few who have assisted in this team project.

Graham George (archaeology and geology), Anthony Cheke (ornithology), Irene Vassalou (culture, history and religious matters), Nikos Vassalos (culture, history and route information), Vangelis Vassalos (culture, history and herbs), Nikolaos Dendrinos (culture and history), Nikitas Giannakopoulos (culture, history and route information), Anna Stebbing (culture and history), Carolina Matthews (history, culture and proofreading), Papa Spirithon and all the priests of Amorgos (inspiration and religious matters), The Mayor of Amorgos; Vice Admiral Nikolaos Fostieris and his council (efforts in restricting building development, dedication to eco-tourism and the protection of paths), John Williams of Everoak web design (IT services), Dudley der Parthog of Sunvil Greece (encouragement and promotion), Tassos Anastassiou[1] , (initiative for and implementation of walking routes in the Cyclades) Vasilis Savvas, Ioannis Prasinos and Panagiotis Psyhogios (maintenance of the protected paths of Amorgos), Panagiotis and Theodore Nomikos and family (culture and history), Penelope Matsouka of Anavasi (cartography). Last, but not least, our publisher Richard Nicholls.

Dedicated to the warm and friendly people of Amorgos, without whom this guide would not have been possible.

---

[1] See appendix: Bibliography

Langada

FOREWORD
by Peter Hughes

Serendipity, like sunshine, can make a holiday. And like sunshine it comes out of the blue.

The word is joyous in every syllable. Coined from a Persian fairytale about the travels of the Princes of Serendip, it's defined as "the faculty for making fortunate discoveries by accident." Interpreters say it's one of the hardest words in English to translate. For me it's easy. It was Amorgos.

I came to the island with my late and much loved partner. She was a Grecophile and, while not so obsessive as to make a tick-list of islands, she was, like other lovers of Greece, on an eternal quest to find her favourite. Amorgos was the last Greek island she visited and one of the most memorable – wild, mountainous, still very Greek and with the priceless advantage for travel romantics of having no airport. All islands are best approached by boat.

Nor was it well known. That alone amounted to serendipity.

Then we met Paul and Henrietta Delahunt-Rimmer, a couple who not only lived on Amorgos, but had explored every cranny of the place. They were as familiar with the island as locals, yet could view it with the perspective of outsiders. For me, a journalist, to stumble upon so rare a cache of insight and expertise was serendipitous in the extreme, especially as much of Amorgos is only really accessible to those who know their mule tracks.

Now Paul and Henri have distilled much of that knowledge into this book. It's worth going to Amorgos just to make use of it. Few guides to any destination impart such a wealth of intimate information. Before you ever lace up your walking boots – which is what the book is really about - look at the background sections on the island past and present. This is not the stuff of academic research but comes direct from people whose families go back to the time of Ariadne. It's the kind of inside gen that, if confided by a villager in a cafeneion, would make your entire holiday worthwhile. And here it is. Just turn the page. Serendipity.

Peter Hughes was the founding editor of ITV's holiday series Wish You Were Here...? and is a prize-winning travel writer who has reported from nearly 130 countries. In 2009 he was honoured in the UK Travel Press Awards for his Outstanding Contribution to Travel Journalism.

Picking Horta

Preface

This guide book is for discerning visitors to the island who are interested in learning about the 'real' Amorgos. The authors introduced walking tours to the island in 1999 and have established it as a primary destination in the Greek islands for walkers. After many years of guiding clients and even local people to some of the amazing sights described they now reveal all. This book takes you to hidden places never previously recorded or seen by visitors without guides - hidden coves, crystal deposits, caves, Neolithic mines, ruined villages and unlisted 6,500 year old archaeological sites, to name just a few of the 'secrets' of the 'Secret Jewel'. This work is the culmination of fifteen years of exploration with the support of historians, archaeologists, geologists, academics and goatherds. It describes the geography, history and geology of the island. The culture, flora and fauna are covered extensively. It contains many anecdotes about island life never before published and through countless years of research and interviews with the islanders it really gets to the heart of the island, its culture and the people. Interspersed amongst the text are excerpts from 'Out of the Rat Race into the Fire' the story of the authors relocating from the comforts of rural life in England to a Spartan and remote existence in the mountains with no amenities or even a road. A Royal Air Force pilot to Royalty and a nursing sister and Air Traffic Control Officer turning to a way of life even the islanders would no longer consider 'sane'.

Pressing Olives

Ellias' olive press was one of the very few remaining old presses in use on the island and a real piece of industrial archaeology. It is located in a small barn, which is blackened with the soot from the open fires used to boil the water for the process. Each family took their olives to him in clearly marked sacks and when he had acquired enough to offer some economies of scale he started the process. Taking each family's batch in turn he tipped them onto a large raised stone circle about 5 feet across and spread them out. A large stone roller pivoted in the centre of the circle was then rotated around to crush the olives. This was driven around by a donkey harnessed to the wooden arm through the centre of the roller. This pulp was then scooped out and placed in a large trough. Boiling water was poured in and was all mixed together into a paste. Donkey hair blankets were then laid on the side and the paste shovelled onto these, which were then folded over to form a square parcel. This package was then placed under a large cast iron press that was wound down by hand to press out all the liquid from the paste. This liquid, a mixture of oil and water ran along a channel under the stone floor into a shallow pit. The oil and water were left to separate and the oil scooped off the top into tins, the water remaining in a sump at the bottom of the pit. The oil was then given back to the families minus a percentage that the press owner kept as payment for the service. The cakes of pressed olives were removed from the blankets and dried. These were then fed to the donkeys, presumably the one doing all the work got the first choice, although he did prefer it when they used the press to process grapes! It is not so traditional these days. EU regulations say that oily water can't be allowed to run down the street. All the olives now go to a boring mechanical press. It is more efficient but not as colourful.

Out of the Rat Race into the Fire

Until 1998, before the road was completed, many villages and settlements were very isolated and only connected by mule tracks or journeys around the coast by boat. It is only by using these tracks that visitors can get to see most places of interest. This guide through careful research and precise directions using GPS reference points (optional) and the accurate maps enclosed directs the reader to areas rarely visited by tourists. Although some long walks are described, many have shorter options which are very easy. This is a guide book for the hidden places on Amorgos as well as many that are easily accessible.

Amorgos is split into three well defined areas dictated by the three ancient city states which were established around the 7th Century BC and had continuous occupation until medieval times. They are Arkesini to the south, Minoa in the centre and Vigla to the north. These areas are now known as Kato Meria (lower land), Chora (city) and Aegiali respectively. The guide is divided into these three distinct districts. Readers can dip into the book and select places of interest to them and either go on extensive walks to these or just walk a short distance from the road to find these hidden places. You may feel energetic enough to push a little further on to the next little gem over the horizon. You can take recommended short cuts or just simply retrace your footsteps when you have walked far enough. Flexibility is the aim of this guide. There are also many places of interest described that can be explored with very little effort such as the villages, many churches and the world famous monastery of Hozoviotissa. You could even just lie on the beach or sit in a cafeneion and read the many humorous stories of island life or learn about the history and places of interest. Everything you need to enjoy an informative visit to Amorgos is contained within this one volume.

X

Taxman

The old days were quite a worry for the shop and taverna owners, especially with the compulsory introduction of tills. If the till breaks down it can take weeks to send it back to Athens for repair or replacement. During this time everything has to be done manually and the Greek regulations for business ownership makes Queen's Regulations in the military look like the guidelines for running a Brownie troop. One, fortunately punctilious, restaurant owner had a major till malfunction in the middle of a very busy lunch period. There was paper everywhere, tempers were frayed and a particularly difficult couple who seemed to be extremely over dressed for the occasion were insisting on a receipt. A manual one was produced with abject apologies for the format and the reason explained. It really was his lucky day; not only did he pass this Taxman's spot inspection with flying colours but there was nothing that these two didn't know about the internal workings of the dreaded cash machine. The till was fixed within minutes instead of weeks and they were on their way, smiles all round. The short delay in their departure, whilst fixing the machine, presumably also gave time to activate the island jungle telegraph and the whole island was in the taxman's good books. Quite a few ouzos were drunk that evening and they certainly didn't go through the books.

Out of the Rat Race into the Fire

Introduction

Amorgos lies 220 km to the south east of Athens. The nearest large islands are Santorini to the south west, Ios to the west and Naxos to the north west all of which are visible from Amorgos on a clear day. Amorgos is the most easterly island in the Cyclades and the seventh largest. It is long and narrow orientated SW to NE 30 km long and between 2.5 and 8 km wide with a coastline of 115 km. The coastline is very dramatic with cliffs in places rising over 700m above sea level. The landscape is mountainous with fertile valleys lying between the mountain ranges. This rugged coastline results in very few areas which open up into bays; the bays that do exist are predominantly along the northern coast, the most accessible being in Katapola and the magnificent long beach in Aegiali. The highest point on the island is Krikelos, to the north, which is 823m high. There are no rivers flowing all year round on the island but in heavy rains the watercourses flow down from the mountains into the sea. The two largest river beds are Varmas, south west of Katapola, which flows into Agii Saranda and Araklos in the north which leads into the bay of Aegiali.

Geologically Amorgos is very interesting. Its origin is completely different to any of the other islands in the Cyclades. It is formed of layers of sedimentary rock of which the oldest were formed 230 million years ago and the most recent about 40 million years ago. It came into its present form about 700,000 years ago as a result of vertical tectonic movements. Indeed, tectonic activity still continues today. There was an earthquake on 9th July 1956 which measured 7.5 on the Richter scale. Apart from the damage to buildings this resulted in fissures in the rock causing many springs to disappear. There are areas on the island which were previously very fertile but after this earthquake they lost their water and became relatively barren. This had a significant effect on fruit production. The majority of the geological structure of the island is limestone and flysh. Much of the flysh is composed of slate. As a result of this all the resources for building are naturally available on the island and it is only in relatively recent times that building materials have begun to be imported. Wood for roof beams came from the Krikelos[1] forest which burnt down in 1835.

The weather on Amorgos is unique in the Cyclades due to the geomorphological features of the island. Its orientation dictates that air masses reaching the area are affected differently to that on other nearby islands. It is the driest of all the islands receiving approximately only 340mm of rainfall a year. This doesn't mean that Amorgos is barren, indeed quite the opposite. The geological structure stores the winter rains resulting in a green and fertile island covered in flowers in the spring. The east/west orientation of the 800m high mountain ridge results in moisture forming by orographic lifting in the prevailing northerly meltemi summer winds. Consequently, the autumn bulbs flower in the late summer before even the first rains have arrived. Greece is not however, 'summer all year around' as some tour operators would wish you to believe. On Amorgos is not unknown to be able to lie in the sun on the beach on Christmas day. However it is also not unknown for there to be a covering of snow on said beach in February. It is nevertheless, a long dry summer with many hours of sunshine.

Mean annual weather conditions for Amorgos

Average	Jan	Feb	Mar	Apr	May	Jun	Jul	Aug	Sep	Oct	Nov	Dec
Max	14°C	14°C	16°C	19°C	22°C	26°C	27°C	26°C	25°C	21°C	19°C	16°C
Min	9°C	9°C	10°C	12°C	15°C	19°C	22°C	22°C	20°C	17°C	13°C	11°C
Mean	12°C	12°C	13°C	16°C	19°C	23°C	25°C	24°C	23°C	19°C	16°C	14°C
Max	57°F	57°F	61°F	66°F	72°F	79°F	81°F	79°F	77°F	70°F	66°F	61°F
Min	48°F	48°F	50°F	53°F	59°F	66°F	72°F	72°F	68°F	63°F	55°F	52°F
Mean	54°F	54°F	55°F	61°F	66°F	73°F	77°F	75°F	73°F	66°F	61°F	57°F
Sun/hrs	90	90	150	180	240	330	390	360	300	180	90	90
Rain	70mm	60mm	45mm	15mm	8mm	2mm	1mm	2mm	3mm	29mm	45mm	60mm

The above chart is for guideline purposes only and does not guarantee actual conditions.

[1] See walk 2

History

The island of Amorgos is steeped in history dating back to the Neolithic period (4,500 – 3,000 BC) and by the Early Cycladic Period (3,000 - 2,000 BC) was a flourishing and important centre with many contacts including Troy and Crete. In the later part of the Cycladic Period Amorgos was dominated by Crete, which resulted in a decline in the local culture as it was replaced by Minoan styles. In the 10th – 8th centuries BC settlers from Naxos built Arkesini, and in the 7th century BC settlers from Samos settled on Minoa, and from Miletus on Vigla. The famous poet Simonides from Samos settled on Amorgos because it was considered by him to be the centre of Greek civilisation. The Archaic Period (7 – 6th Centuries BC) saw the development of the three 'city states', and widening contact with Samos and Paros. The Classical Period (5 – 4th centuries BC) saw increasing domination from first Athens, and then Alexander the Great, when the three cities flourished and minted their own coinage on the island of Nikouria. Indeed, despite domination Amorgos managed to remain essentially independent due to its isolation up until the Roman occupation of Greece in 168BC. Amorgos prospered at this time due to an increase in agricultural production, particularly in olive oil and wine. Its remote and inaccessible location also made Amorgos a favourite place to be sent into exile; far away enough not to cause trouble and with the benefit of being able to survive easily.

The Byzantine era (AD 324 – 1207) was one of many raids by Goths, Vandals[1], Arabs and Venetians, with the islanders being left largely to fend for themselves. The pirates not only raided but also settled in some ports, including Katapola, and used them as bases. Towers, old and new, were used as defence points and hiding places. Crops and animals were hidden in caves and church crypts. Large areas of land remained uncultivated. Friendly relations were fostered with the pirates and Amorgos again became prosperous and thickly populated. Amorgos also became a favoured place of exile for Byzantine officers, including General Vroutsis, after whom the village of Vroutsi[2] is named.

The Venetian Occupation (1207 – 1537) saw the island becoming a dependency of Naxos when seized by Geronimo and Andrea Gizi. The Chora was fortified with the keep being built on top of the rock. By the 14th century Moslem raids from Asia Minor had become fiercer and more frequent, resulting in the island being almost abandoned on at least three occasions. The land became ruined and neglected, and animals either slaughtered or stolen. Men had been kidnapped to crew pirate ships and children had been abducted and sold as slaves.

Amorgos was captured by the Ottomans, lead by Barbarossa, in 1537 and this started the Ottoman occupation which lasted until Greece was finally free in 1824.During this period the Ottomans were more interested in land rather than sea power, and showed little interest in the islands apart from extracting heavy taxes from them. The islanders were mostly indifferent to their new master except

---

[1] This tribe being the origin of the modern term 'vandalism'
[2] See Walk 9

that the Turks were marginally better than the Venetians who had done little to ingratiate themselves. This was another period of declining agriculture and population, with most people living inland in the mountains and fleeing regularly to mountain hideouts. While Amorgos enjoyed the benefits of religious freedom enabling them to repair and build churches, piracy still remained their greatest danger. Amorgos became an important centre and became economically dependent on the pirates for business. One positive advantage was that many Greeks learnt how to fight at sea and piracy encouraged the growth of Greek seamanship. Many young men from Amorgos fought in the Greek War of Independence of 1821.

Independence and the formation of the Kingdom of Greece saw improved conditions for the islanders and an expansion of agriculture due to improved technology and skills. Amorgos was self-sufficient and exported many products including wine, olive oil, cotton, silk, timber and tobacco. A regular, weekly steamship service transported coal, pottery and animals as well as people around the Small Cyclades. In 1828 the monks from the monastery set up the secondary school in Chora, which was the first in the Cyclades. However, despite their efforts literacy still remained low as most children were needed to work the land. Medical services were improved with the arrival of doctors and a midwife. The doctors and midwife were also responsible for the small islands and would travel by caique when needed. Every day the doctor would walk up to the windmills above Langada to look for signals; one fire for a doctor, two fires if the case was urgent and three fires if the police were needed as well! More foreign visitors arrived despite Amorgos' reputation for being remote due to its dangerous coastline and lack of security. In 1857 the German archaeologist Ludwig Ross established the location of the three ancient cities as well as visiting Agia Triada tower. The British writer, James Theodore Bent[1] spent Easter week in 1885 travelling around the island and even today his written account is interesting reading. The Greek Cypriote Miliarakis visited in 1879 and reported that the island, although becoming more dry and barren, was still able to produce enough for the needs of the population and export. Piracy was just about eliminated by the end of the 19th century; the steamer ships were large and armed making attack more difficult and dangerous for the pirates and ensured piracy ceased to pay.

The Second World War saw Amorgos occupied by Italian soldiers from Rhodes on May 2nd 1941. Many young men escaped to Egypt and fought in the Greek army and navy. Those left behind suffered acute shortages as much of their produce was commandeered despite food being hidden. Caiques from Amorgos were sometimes able to take supplies to relatives in Athens and bring back news of loved ones. However in the autumn of 1943, German soldiers from Naxos replaced the Italian soldiers and the islanders were forbidden to take any boats out of harbour, even to fish. It is said that some people died of starvation that winter and the locals say that many more would have died if they hadn't had supplies of olive oil.

---

[1] See appendix: Bibliography

Sunset behind Langada

Megali Glyfada[1]

It is here during the Italian occupation during WWII that a British commando vessel hid. They couldn't be seen from the sea and apart from the very remote spot where we were standing they couldn't be seen from the land. It was a near perfect hiding place. They didn't however bank on the goatherds tending their animals in these almost inaccessible places. They also didn't allow for the generosity of the islanders even when times were very hard and their propensity for partying. As soon as Nikitas' father and family saw the boat they gathered freshly baked bread, home produced cheese and goats milk and raki and went down to greet their allies. No amount of persuasion would stop them from throwing a party on the beach. When the British were finally persuaded that there was no chance on earth that the Italians would find them there they joined the islanders on the beach. Out came the violins and lautos and the singing and dancing lasted three days. No one, of course, found out what the commandos were doing there or what their mission was but they seemed to enjoy their three days of unofficial R&R. Now there is no one in the bay and no one on the beach, not even a German towel in sight. It looks like an impossible task to make your way down the sides of the gorge but Nikitas showed us the start of a hidden path where they used to take their donkeys down.

Out of the Rat Race into the Fire

6

The post war period saw little improvement and severe shortages prevailed. There was still no steamer service so the islanders had to rely on the occasional caique passing through for some supplies. Many young people left the island and did not return, leaving behind an ageing population dependent on farming and fishing. Many buildings, including the schools were in a parlous state. The secondary school was threatened with closure due to lack of money, teachers and children. The Abbot of the monastery gave money to enable the school to remain open and also set up the hostel in Chora to accommodate boys from other villages and islands. Girls were encouraged to attend secondary school for the first time as well

Shark Fishing

The Pagali Hotel, where our clients stay, is an 'Agritourist' Hotel. That is to say it is primarily a farming company and the hotel and taverna is related diversification. This works out very well as much of the food is from their own farm. Nikos, the owner, insists on all his products being organic so, of course, most of the dishes at the hotel are organic. The pork, chicken, eggs, salads and vegetables are all organic and grown on Amorgos. All the waste from the kitchen apart from the meat goes back to the animals and so the cycle starts again. He also has a fishing boat that helps to supplement the farm produce. His favourite quarry is shark, with the record so far a five metre, two hundred and seventy five kilo, five gilled shark. This was longer than his boat. Obviously it was too large to go inside so it had to be towed half way around the island to Aegiali. He didn't have a harpoon or shotgun with him to kill it. They managed to get its chin onto the stern but obviously it wasn't very happy and was thrashing and gnashing dangerously, threatening to turn the boat over. The only way to control it was to get a rope around the tail and pull this onto the stern as well. There was only Nikos and his godfather, also a Nikos, on board. The whole operation took over three hours. When we saw it we couldn't believe what they had achieved. The following day he wanted to go out and find a bigger one but no one would go with him.

Out of the Rat Race into the Fire

---

[1] See walk three

Ormos Aegialis

as the young men who had fought in the war. The island was without a doctor until 1954 and even then all medicines had to come from Naxos, taking a week to arrive. On 9th July 1956 Amorgos suffered a severe earthquake; 7.5 on the Richter scale. This prodded the government into action; cement was provided to repair the schools, a shipping service was re-established, electricity and piped water was provided in Chora, the quay was built in Katapola and the road connecting Katapola and Chora was built. In the years of the military Junta (1967-1974) Amorgos again became a popular place to exile criminals and out of favour politicians, the most famous being George Mylonas, exiled to Chora, in 1968 who made a spectacular escape by boat the following year.

In more modern times, 1982 saw the building of the quay in Aegiali and the arrival of electricity there. The main roads serving all the main villages and linking Aegiali, Katapola and Kato Meria were started in 1983 and finally completed in 1998.

In the 1800s the population of Amorgos was about 5,000. In the census of 1991 it was 1,500 and in the census of 2001 it had risen to 1,800. In recent years Amorgos has adapted to modern times and the increase in tourism whilst maintaining its traditional personality. Many islanders continue to live a traditional lifestyle, alongside more modern occupations which have encouraged younger people to stay.

An old photograph of Manolis

Our Local Ship

There was another occasion when the old Skopelitis was running very late due to a family relocation. Mother, father and two children with all their worldly possessions were on board to be moved to a remote island without even a quay. The ship was anchored off-shore and rugs, chairs, kettles, beds, clothes and farming implements were all handed down to a small rowing boat and shuttled to the shore. After a considerable length of time the operation was complete, farewells were exchanged and the ferry eventually set off again. After a few minutes a very observant passenger noticed the rowing boat heading after them at a speed that would do a University Boat team proud, someone was standing in the bows waving and shouting. Captain Skopelitis was informed and yet again the ferry came to a halt, the boat pulled along side, the forgotten toddler was handed over and everyone continued on their way again.

Out of the Rat Race into the Fire

Culture

Traditionally the people of Amorgos lived within a 'closed' rural family economy based on self-sufficiency and selling or bartering any surplus. Their houses were built of stone and mud with a flat roof, which collected rainwater that was then stored in cisterns. Apart from a few springs these water cisterns provided the family and farm with water for the whole year and thus had to be used economically. Water was drawn by bucket and in the house poured into a container with a tap to provide 'running' water for washing. Soap was made from the remains of olive oil production. The house usually consisted of a kitchen with storeroom and a main living room with a raised bed in an alcove. Cooking would be done on a wood fire in a small fireplace and the charcoal put into a brazier to provide heat. Oil lamps and beeswax candles provided light. There would be a covered courtyard with a large oven, water cistern and sometimes a wine press. Most of the farming was on the terraced fields, which had been made as early as the 5th century BC. The terraced fields required constant maintenance to ensure they would not collapse and continue to retain water. Olive trees were planted so that their roots would prevent soil erosion and enable the farmer to grow crops on the land.

With only basic tools available, and with the help of donkeys and mules, farming the land necessitated a large amount of manual labour for all. Ploughing a field involved a donkey pulling a plough, which was guided by one man. Due to the stony nature of the land any large stones had to be moved manually. The sowing of

Water Supply

The water at our house in Stroumbos is collected off the flat roofs in the torrential rains of the winter and runs into two storage tanks underneath two patios. One is actually the old bread oven and cobbler's shop that has been sealed up for this storage purpose. On top of each tank is a well cover, which, when opened will allow a bucket to be dropped down to lift up the water. This water is then poured into small semi cylindrical tanks that fit onto the wall with a little brass tap at the bottom. Our shower is gravity fed from a small tank on the roof which in the winter fills from the rain and in summer has to be topped up by climbing onto the roof with the well bucket. In the summer the tank heats up in the sun and you have a hot shower. In the winter it doesn't and you don't! When showering you stand in a large bowl and collect all the water, which along with all laundry water, is used to flush the loo. Any water used for cooking that is left over is used for washing up. That water subsequently goes onto the plants and shrubs around the patios and in the small garden. One small problem with the latter operation is that when the inevitable teaspoon gets left in the bottom of the bowl it is ends up on the plants. When you realise that you are getting short of teaspoons you have to search around in all the terracotta pots and under shrubs to bring the kitchen inventory back into line. To someone living with piped water, electricity, mains drainage and a water heating system this may sound quite a palaver. It actually takes very little time to adapt to this discipline and it is the way that the islanders have lived for thousands of years and many still do today. With the constant threat of water shortages in Europe a lot can be learnt from this way of living.

Out of the Rat Race into the Fire

Distilling Raki

seeds was done by hand, as was any watering and harvesting. Crops included a mixture of barley and wheat; hedging their chances with the unpredictable rainfall they were guaranteed some crop, as wheat favoured lots of water while barley grew well in dry conditions. Threshing involved a row of donkeys trampling over the crop and winnowing was done manually. The grain would then be transported by donkey to the family windmill or to someone else's to be milled. Traditionally the family bread oven would be lit once a month and a large quantity of bread made. Most of the bread was then sliced and put back into the cooling oven to bake into rusks. These were stored in ceramic jars covered with a stone and provided the family with bread for the rest of the month. Some crops such as tomatoes and cucumbers were planted in a deep hole and given a lot of water and then covered. As the plant grew the stalk was covered with soil to encourage the plant to grow one very strong long root thus negating the need for any further watering. Animals such as chickens, pigs, cattle, and goats would provide eggs, milk, cheese and meat. Fruits would be eaten fresh and any surplus such as tomatoes and figs would be sun dried. Olives were picked by hand and pressed using a donkey and then two strong men. Olives for eating were stored for two weeks in rock salt and then in brine and vinegar. Grapes were handpicked with some sun-dried and the rest were pressed by foot to make wine and retsina. The remains of the grapes were used to distil raki, which was illegal and done in strict secrecy. Honey for sweets either came from their own bees or from collecting from wild bees. Some crops were grown commercially for export such as fava, cotton and tobacco.

The Olive Pickers

The olive tree, if God's gift to the Mediterranean people, was not a gift of manna. It was however constructed in such a way that with a little contrivance the clusters which seem most elusive somehow can be picked. The main branches are steady for climbing, often horizontal, and the smaller ones resilient, you can catch them with the handle of a walking stick, tie, tug and bind them down. Where the olives are many the picking of the dangling tips resembles milking, fingers work together and the olives rain onto the sackcloth spread beneath. When there are few one throws them patiently down one by one. But where the olives grow right above the trunk or a tree grows over a wall the sackcloth is useless and then you use an olive-picker's apron tied tightly around the waist and attached with hooks or strings to two carefully selected branches to form an outstretched bag. Then you can pull down the olive-laden branches and when these are prolific stand in one position for an hour working systematically through what is within reach until the bag is heavy and ready to be emptied out with care. If one side slips there is a ghastly moment when the olives fall into a gorse bush; the catastrophe of a second is a prickly and tedious one to the right.

'The Olive Pickers' by Carola Matthews. The Cornhill Magazine Summer 1974.

Raki

Do you actually know what Raki, or Tsipouro is? If you have drunk it you probably can't remember or were past caring! Essentially it is a strong distilled spirit usually produced from the must-residue of the wine press (pomace). Thus, it is an autumn activity. The name is dependant upon the area it comes from. In Turkey Raki has an aniseed flavour like Greek Ouzo whereas Raki in Greece has no additives. It is just plain rocket fuel containing approximately 45 percent alcohol by volume. The strength can vary enormously depending upon the temperature it is distilled at. Although history is a little vague it appears to have been started by Greek Orthodox monks – well it would be wouldn't it! Records indicate that it was first produced during the 14th century on Mount Athos in Macedonia.

A considerable amount of Raki is made on small scales on Amorgos. A considerable amount of Raki is also consumed on Amorgos. After making the wine the pomace is put into large barrels and water added at a ratio of 70% 'gunge' and 30% water. These are sealed up and left for a month in the sun to ferment.

The fermented pomace is placed in a copper boiler heated from underneath, traditionally with a fire from the prunings of the vines. The boiler has a long copper funnel which passes through barrels filled with cold water. As the hot steam is cooled it condenses and liquidates. In approximately an hour, the warm Raki begins to fall, drop by drop, on the other side of the funnel. This lasts for many hours, during which the owners of the boilers must taste for alcohol content, increase or decrease the heat and finally stop distillation when the raki has acquired the desired taste and strength. We always try to be on hand to assist with this arduous task and keep the distiller awake. The donkeys are still recovering from the time a certain person fell asleep and the raki all overflowed into their field.

Special Interest Holidays Newsletter Dec 2009

Fishing caiques were made of wood in Katapola and rowed using two narrow wooden oars with the rower facing the bow. Fishing was either with nets or a row of hooks on a long line. Octopus was caught using one large hook. Families would usually have their own small caique for fishing or, if not, the villagers would wait for the fishermen to visit the villages with their fish on a donkey. The fisherman would blow a conch shell horn to announce his arrival. Transport between the small islands and often even between Aegiali and Katapola was by caique carrying people, coal, pottery and animals. Once a week a steamship travelled between the island and Athens. As there was no quay the steamship would anchor in the bay and people transported to and from the ship by caique. Large animals such as bulls had to swim to the ship where they were winched on board by ropes tied to their horns and legs.

Cotton and hand woven wool would be used to weave colourful textiles. In ancient times Amorgos produced its own silk, dyed using Amorgian flax and made into very fine purple tunics, which were very much sought after. The women would decorate their clothes with silk embroidery and make white cotton scarves and silk gloves for working in the fields. Reeds would be used for basket weaving and large ceramic pots were made for storage. The carpenter would make anything from doors and tables to donkey saddles. The forge provided metal tools for the farmers and buckets for the women. Leather goods such as shoes were bought and repaired at the cobblers.

Villagers celebrating the revived festival of Kapitanios

Communication was very basic with no roads, telephones or television. Twice a week the town clerk would walk through the village calling out the news. On Saturdays the shipping timetables and auctions would be announced. When the auction actually took place the ringing of the church bells signalled its start. The arrival of the steamship was more unpredictable; people would travel to the port to await its arrival and on many occasions camped out in the only cafeneion for days! The postman, using two donkeys, delivered the post. On his arrival at the first house of the village he would give three blasts from his whistle and then four blasts on reaching the village square. Not only would post be delivered but also the latest news from the steamship and more importantly the names of any new arrivals.

Even up until recent times village life was very simple with most families living off the land. The women would look after home and family and it was the women who would make the twice-weekly trip to Chora and back ferrying their children to the secondary school. The children would either stay in the hostel there or in rented accommodation. The men would relax and swap stories in the village cafeneion. In the 1970's a few cafeneions invested in petrol driven generators to run refrigerators. While these generators were noisy one of the benefits was the introduction of the television. Women for the first time spent time in the cafeneion joining in with this new novelty. The introduction of a telephone improved communication with the outside world but also improved the bush telegraph as appointments had to be made to receive and make calls and the telephonist always listened in!

Whilst the introduction of the road, electricity and telecommunications have improved the living conditions for the islanders and brought many benefits, it has not changed their basic way of life; the traditions continue to this day. Despite numerous islanders now making their living running pensions and shops, many still farm on a market garden scale; various fresh fruits and vegetables are available either from the gardens themselves or from the owner travelling around the villages with his produce on a donkey. The local fishermen still visit the villages and blow their shell 'horns' to announce their arrival; the only difference being that he has a van to transport the fish. Products such as wine, eggs and honey are all still produced and available locally. Carpenters continue to make all sorts of furniture, doors and donkey saddles. Donkeys are still very much used for carrying all sorts of goods around the countryside and the villages, and agriculture is still very manual regardless of the introduction of rotavators and olive picking machines. Despite more modern occupations many islanders are still practically self-sufficient for food. The post is still delivered to the villages and distributed in certain shops or cafeneions. Modern plumbing and piped water has not stopped the islanders collecting rainwater and being extremely frugal with its use. And, most importantly, the men still spend hours in the many traditional cafeneions swapping stories and gossip!

Entertainment

With no television, computers or DVD's entertainment was traditionally 'homemade'. Women would spend hours on handicrafts including making embroidery and lace. The men would spend hours in the cafeneion playing cards or tavli and putting the world to rights and telling each other stories and gossip. Travelling players and musical and theatrical groups provided extra entertainment. A travelling puppet theatre would visit the cafeneions with the children sitting on the floor to watch. On special occasions local musicians would and still do play the violin and lauto and sing traditional songs. Many of these songs are very old and frequently adapted to the moment and situation. Even to this day on special occasions the locals will dress in traditional outfits and perform Greek folk dances.

The two weeks before the start of Lent are known as carnival and is the time for partying before the period of fasting starts. In the past dances took place in cafeneions at the weekends with local orchestras playing. The last Saturday culminated in a masked dance with groups of people called mandeldes or mascari dressed in disguise going from house to house having fun; a tradition which still happens. On the last Sunday of Lent the village of Langada celebrated a pagan festival called Kapitanios. This festival is unique to the island of Amorgos and not practiced anywhere else in Greece. In 1998 this was revived after a break of twenty -five years. A young single man from Aegiali is voted to be Kapitanios and after a ceremony at the church of Panagia he rides through the village platea on a mule. The young single ladies of Aegiali dance in the platea to traditional music dressed in colourful costumes and the Kapitanios selects his maid. This is the last party before the start of Lent which starts the next day and is known as Clean Monday. Traditionally this is the day when the women cleaned all the cooking pots and implements so that there was no contamination when preparing fasting foods. Many people still fast at this time and despite many limitations lobster is still allowed to be on the menu! Many families enjoy the Bank holiday and take their children into the countryside to fly kites, which were traditionally made of bamboo and coloured paper.

Greek Orthodox Easter (Paska)

Paska is a time for celebrations and festivities that surpass even the most lavish of Christmas revelry anywhere in the world. Paska is calculated using a different calendar to the Catholic Church and the two can be up to five weeks apart. Greek families travel from all over the world to get together in their home villages in an incredible atmosphere with fireworks and feasting. Some of the islands, particularly Amorgos, are inconceivably special at this time of year because of the traditional way of life and all the spring flowers are at their very best. The flowers and herbs carpet the hillsides in a spectacular show of colour.

Some islands are quieter than others, some are almost impossible to get to, and on other more traditional and remote ones such as Amorgos the islanders get completely carried away and throw fire crackers and even sticks of dynamite to punctuate the activities. The island's three distinct communities are all brought together in the festivities. Three invaluable and treasured gold Byzantine icons are kept in the main monastery of Hozoviotissa. On Easter Sunday a priest will lead a procession with one of these icons to each district. Unlike many places in Greece where this transfer is done by road, on Amorgos they parade for hours through the mountains, on the old donkey tracks, accompanied by the islanders on donkeys singing and playing traditional instruments as they proceed. Many remote villages are included in the tour and services are held in all the main churches and many small chapels on route.

The sombre mood of Holy week intensifies as Saturday approaches. On Good Friday at sunset a service is held in each of the large village churches. Half way through the service the congregation come out of church and a procession goes around the village led by the priest and the villagers carrying a bier on which there is an effigy of Christ. When they get back to the church the bier is held up high and everyone processes underneath it back into church for the second half of the service.

Saturday is a quiet day in the village square but behind closed doors and in the narrow streets the lady of the house has her busiest day of the year. It is her job to prepare the family feast for Easter Sunday. Throughout Holy Week shots are heard in the mountains, as the Goat Herds shoot young kids (goats not children!) for Easter and now is the time for them to be prepared. The village streets are not a place for the squeamish on Easter Saturday. If the kids were caught alive they are

Monastery

Three of the five silver eikons in the church were to be the object of our veneration for seven days to come. One adorns a portrait of the Madonna herself, found, they say, by some sailors in the sea below, in two pieces, in which condition it was washed all the way from Cyprus, having been treated profanely there. It is beautifully embossed with silver and gold, as are also the other eikons. This fashion of fulfilling a vow by putting a silver arm or limb on a sacred picture has had a curious effect on the general appearance, and reminds us of the statue mentioned by Lucian which Eucrates had in his house, and had gilded the breast as a thank-offering for recovery from a fever. A second is of St. George Balsamitis, the patron saint of the prophetic source of Amorgos, of which more anon; and another is an iron cross, set in silver, and found, they say, on the heights of Mount Krytelos, a desolate mountain to the north of Amorgos, only visited by peasants, who go there to cut down the prickly evergreen oak which covers it, as fodder for their mules.

Bent, James Theodore. 1885. *The Cyclades or Life among the Insular*

slaughtered and dealt with quite openly. They are hung up in doorways to skin and clean and their intestines are also hung up, kept aside to make the traditional Easter soup. It is an acquired taste and traditionalists say the best soup comes from intestines that are not cleaned! Not recommended for the uninitiated. There are two ways of cooking the kid. The most common preparation these days is spit roast over a charcoal fire, which is done on Amorgos manually in the street. All you can smell on Easter Sunday is the wonderful aroma of roasting goat, liberally covered in herbs from the mountains, wafting through the villages. You will be offered pieces from the family's Easter roast as you pass; such is the friendliness and kind-hearted approach of these people. The other way to cook the kid, which is more traditional, is stuffed with rice, spinach and herbs and put it in the baker's oven overnight. Whichever way you wish it is just wonderful, and similar to very tender lamb.

At sunset on Easter Saturday the villagers start to gather in the square at the tavernas and the atmosphere is electric. This is the build up to the biggest moment of the year for everyone. Just before midnight everyone files into the church and the liturgy begins. At midnight it reaches its climax with the words, 'Christ is risen' the sombre mood of the past week is shattered by peals of bells and exploding fireworks. Everyone in the congregation and people in the street will turn to each other and say, 'He is truly risen'. This statement and response will be heard many times as people greet each other over the following week. The service continues for a little while after Midnight. However on one occasion a few years ago, on Amorgos, it came to an abrupt end when the whole village had to rush out of church to extinguish a bush fire started by a slightly over-enthusiastic young man throwing sticks of dynamite.

If everything goes according to plan the congregation and priest gather outside the church after the service and the church doors are closed. The priest holds a candle with the holy flame and calls for all the evil spirits to leave the church. Theoretically the doors of the church should miraculously fly open and the evil spirits disperse. In practice someone is left inside to perform this task. Some years ago on Amorgos when the priest performed this ceremony the trusted insider, as a joke, didn't open the doors. The priest thinking that he may not have heard shouted the prayers louder and louder until he was blue in the face and, much to the amusement of the crowd, getting extremely annoyed. Needless to say he has not been caught out again, yet.

The crowd light their candles from the priest's holy flame until the whole square is illuminated with flickering light. If people can get back home without their flame going out it is said they will have a good year. On returning home early on Easter Sunday many people break their fast with the soup made from the goats entrails and some even go on to have their main Easter feast. On Amorgos the islanders are renowned throughout the Cyclades for their ability to party for days and in some villages the music and dancing goes on all night.

Different islands and different villages have various traditions over the next two days. In the village of Tholaria on Easter Sunday afternoon they have various games and dancing in the square. It is quite common for some of the elderly men to forget their age and play leapfrog and do some wild dancing with people a quarter of their age. It is also therefore quite common for the doctor to be called the following day when they can't get out of bed. In the village of Langada on Easter Monday afternoon the villagers sit an effigy of Judas on a wall and blast it to pieces with shotguns. The celebrations tail off after this but continue to a small degree for the next forty days. A week after Easter the icons lent to the three parishes are taken in a procession, through the mountains, back to the Hozoviotissa monastery.

Other Festivals[1]

Today's religious festivals are descendants of pre-Christian rituals taking from them the libations, rural parades and the sharing of food with everyone at the same table. Ancient texts describe meat from sacrificial animals being distributed to the table companions. This has evolved into the tradition of serving Patatato which is goat cooked in a large cauldron with potatoes and served to everyone at the same table from the same pot. However, at the larger festivals this dish may be made with pasta or sometimes fish or salted cod is served. Other dishes are also often served along with copious amounts of wine or raki. At smaller chapels bread and cheese is usually served along with wine or retsina. These festivals are performed at the relevant church according to the saint's day being celebrated. Anyone named after that particular saint celebrates their 'name day' by attending the festival and giving out sweets. After the larger festivals parties take place in the nearest village with music and dancing and usually continuing well into the next morning.

Weddings are normally large affairs and start late afternoon. Traditionally the bride arrives at the church by donkey and accompanied by musicians; the groom and bridesmaid wait outside the church and the wedding party then enters church followed by as many guests who can squeeze in. At the end of the service all the guests process into the church to congratulate the happy couple. Following the church service sweets and wine are served and sugared almonds in muslin bags are given as gifts to the guests. Wedding receptions are large and involve a lot of food and dancing and usually continue to early morning or even continue for days! (One wedding party continued for three days and only ended when most of the guests had to catch the ship to Athens) Baptisms are also large affairs and very important to the devout; sometimes families will save for years to provide a large party and all their children will be baptised at the same time. It is not so long ago that the dates of the baptism were used as the date of birth. As some children were quite old when baptised this was not a very accurate record of their age. There are still many of the older generation who do not know exactly how old they are. And, they do not really care!

---

[1] See Appendix

Flowers and Trees

The types of flowers and trees found on Amorgos are dictated by the climate. Winters are mild and moist with temperatures rarely dropping below 5°C whereas the summer is long and dry with no rain for many months. This climate results in plant growth in the cooler months with a profusion of flowers in the spring. In the summer all the plants die or lie dormant and the mountain sides are brown. As soon as there is moisture in the air the autumn bulbs start to flower and after the first rain it only takes one week for everything to turn lush and green again.

Castor Oil Plant (Ricinus communis) Langada

Thousands of years ago much of Amorgos was forested. As man started to populate the island and cultivate the ground the vegetation changed. Trees were cut down for building or fuel. Bushes were cleared to enable the ground to be ploughed to sow crops. To this end much of the natural plant cover is restricted to the more remote areas. Fortunately on Amorgos these areas abound. Also due to significant climate change there have been, over the centuries, many changes in the vegetation. The introduction of goats and other grazing animals to the island has also had a significant effect. However, for wild flower enthusiasts the results of intervention by man on the island has not been totally negative. Many of the most interesting flowers on Amorgos can be found in maquis and garigue. Maquis being scrubland vegetation composed primarily of leathery, broad-leaved evergreen shrubs or small trees. This occurs primarily on the lower slopes of mountains bordering the sea. Many of the shrubs are aromatic, such as mints, laurels, and myrtles. Olives, figs, and other small trees are scattered throughout. Garigue, is a poorer version of this vegetation and is found in areas with a thin, rocky soil.

The olive groves and other cultivated ground are rich in wild flowers. On Amorgos they also benefit from the lack of use of herbicides as organic farming abounds.

Amorgos is very popular with botanists due to the incredible number of species that are found on the island. According to the Flora Hellenica Data base around 600 species exist on the island out of 1,670 in the Cyclades. Some sub species are unique to Amorgos and many are protected[1].

The herbs of Amorgos are famous. The Island is a sensory delight, and the moment that you step off the ship you can smell the herbs. Usually this is your first impression of Amorgos as the scent is carried in the air across the sea to the ship as you approach the island.

The islanders still use these herbs, both fresh and dried, for culinary and medicinal use in addition to making scented combinations to hang in rooms or cupboards. You can pick the herbs yourself and take them home with you or buy products on Amorgos, or indeed all over the world, which are prepared from them. These herbs are the ultimate in organic and natural produce.

Bug Orchid (Orchis coriophora) Araklos Gorge Aegiali

---

[1] See Appendix

Animals, Reptiles and Insects

There are a great number of animals, reptiles and insects on Amorgos including some very rare sub species which are unique to the island. The very first mention however has to go to the Monk seal[1] (*Monachus-Monachus*). This delightful but illusive creature is one of the most endangered mammals in the world with only 350-450 individuals remaining. They are in the waters around Amorgos but a sighting is very rare. This Mediterranean seal used to breed in profusion on remote sandy beaches and in coves. Indeed the old Roman harbour at the end of the beach in Aegiali is called Fokiotripa[2] (seal hole). With the increase in tourism[3] and development of their breeding grounds they have been forced to retreat to caves. In this environment the baby seals are quite often injured by large waves slamming into the entrance. The over fishing of the Mediterranean has also been a cause of their demise.

There are many lizards on the island but one unique to Amorgos is the Amorgos Lizard (*Podarcis erhardii amorgensis*). Another unique reptile is the Amorgos Lafitis (*Elaphe quatuorlineata rechingeri*). This rat snake is very docile and doesn't attack. It is greyish in colour and grows up to 1.3m long and is as thick as a wrist. Many people encourage them to stay around their stables to keep down the rats. Another snake of significance found on Amorgos is the San Boa (*Eryx jaculus turcicus*). There many other species of snake, some are poisonous but most are not. None are deadly. In the heat of the day they usually shelter under rocks or in crevices in walls, so don't pick up rocks or put your hand into any gaps in walls. There are many scorpions of course. These are fairly small and the sting, though unpleasant, is not life threatening. The worst and most feared insect on the island is known locally as the Sarandapothi (forty legs). It is actually the Scolopendromorpha which, according the authors' research, actually has 42 legs but no one here is going to hang around long enough to count them. This bright orange, aggressive, fast moving centipede can grow up to 24cm long and has a very painful bite. It will even prey on lizards. Snakes will eat them and cats seem to be able to kill them without getting bitten. If you take off your shoes in the mountains always shake them out before putting them back on. They just love walking boots, pockets and folds in clothing. If your favourite table is taken in a local taverna on Amorgos just point underneath it and shout, 'sarandapothi' and the table will soon clear, probably along with the whole of the taverna.

On a more pleasant front there are stripe-necked turtles (*Mauremys caspica*), frogs (*Rana ridibunda*) and common old tortoises, rabbits, hares, foxes and pine martins. Many reptiles can be seen during the day but usually you will see more mammals at night.

---

[1] Protected 92/43 E.U. & ibid 3.2d 4.2.
[2] See Walk 1
[3] See Appendix: eco-tourism

Birds

The ornithology[1] on Amorgos is of great interest to bird watchers. There are two rare birds on the island which are almost unique to the area these are Eleonora's Falcon[2] (*Falco eleonorae*) and Bonelli's eagle[2] (*Hieraaetus fasciatus*). The major centre for the Eleonora's Falcon is the Aegean and Amorgos is in the centre of this concentration. There are estimated to be a total population in the world of 18,000. There are now just 10,000 Bonelli's Eagles in the world. The other rare bird occasionally seen on the island is the Audouin's gull (*Laurus Auduinii*) there are about 58,000 in the world but only 800 in Greece and this population is decreasing. It is however difficult to spot the difference between this and the more common Herring/Yellow-legged gulls. As you walk along little used paths you see a great variety of birds which are indigenous to the island. Amorgos is also a transitory stop over for birds migrating from the North to Africa for the winter. You can spend many hours in the spring and autumn watching the antics of the bee eaters as they sweep around the sky in pursuit of their quarry. The most impressive of all however are the eagles (Steppe, Spotted, Lesser Spotted & Asian Imperial). If you are lucky you may see them high in the sky circling in the mountains. The most likely of all of these rare eagle sightings is the Lesser Spotted during the migratory period.

The Bee Eater in Africa

[1] See Appendix
[2] protected 92/43 E.U. & ibid 3.2d 4.2.

Gypsies

The islanders tolerate the gypsies, as they do not cause any trouble, there is no point in them stealing anything as there is nowhere to run to and they do supply goods at a reasonable price. They do however try everything to beg water. The other day they claimed it was to mix the baby's milk. Given that the container held five gallons, I wouldn't like to meet that baby on a dark night in the crèche. On one occasion, Nikos, one of the small taverna owners on the front was watering his plants with a hosepipe. The gypsies must have smelt the fresh water from half a mile away and were there within seconds with their water containers. He had just finished watering and being very generous he lent them the still running hose with instructions to turn it off when they had filled their water bottles. It was like leaving a child in charge of a sweet shop or a matlow in charge of a brewery. Nikos had walked off into the village leaving his bar totally unattended but all they were interested in was the cool fresh water, it was too tempting to resist. There was mother, who was built more like a whaling ship than a whale, her diminutive husband and the three sons. She ordered the sons to strip down to their pants and produced a very large scrubbing brush. Under the running water she then proceeded to scrub them down until their previously sun darkened bodies were pink and shiny, she ignored the screams of pain and the complaints until she was satisfied that their top half's, at least, were spotless. To the amazement of diners nearby she then demanded that they strip completely and oversaw the scrubbing of their nether regions. Obviously they were very embarrassed about this performance, especially given the attention it was getting from passers-by. They did their best to do a rapid and discreet job but mother was having none of it, 'more, more', she screamed. In due course each was inspected and to their relief were announced 'done' and were able to dress again. They got dressed without the help of their parents. This was reasonable, as all three were well into their teens! That evening they were all asleep in a row on the sand at the end of the beach like the contents of sardine tin, all covered with one blanket. Four small humps, and a very large one at the end. It was midnight and a disco had just started at a nearby taverna. Through bleary eyes the four men saw group after group of mini skirted beauties passing by, the lure was too much to resist. One by one they got up and crept off to see the action. Normally their presence would not be welcome due to the pervading odour but this evening was different of course. Although they had no money to buy drinks they were perfectly well accepted just standing there with their mouths wide open ogling the action on the dance floor. All of a sudden one of them shouted out in pain and swung round to see the mother, blotting out the moonlight, brandishing a shoe. She may be large but she is pretty quick with hand weapons managing to clout each of them at least once before they came to their senses. This apparently totally immoral activity of gawping at scantily clad gyrating girls on the dance floor did not meet with her approval. They were escorted back to their sardine tin and ordered back to bed. After a while the large hump of the whaling ship at the end started to sound its foghorn. One by one the four smaller humps started to melt into the sand until all that could be seen was one large black mound, rising and falling in time with the waves lapping on the shore.

Out of the Rat Race into the Fire

Walking

The great beauty of walking on Amorgos is that the island is incredibly diverse and rich in antiquities and sights. Walking in the north and then in the south you would think that you were on a different island. The cliffs and peaks above Langada towards Stavros have been described as 'Alpinistic' whilst the landscape of the south is far less rugged. Before the road was finished these were two very different communities in their way of life and culture. Even today you can detect a difference.

Normal precautions for walking in remote areas should be adhered to. Water is the first priority. Quite often there are no water supplies en route. In the introduction to each walk this aspect is covered. In the spring and autumn it is a good idea to obtain a weather forecast before setting off, even if only by asking one of the local people. When planning a high altitude walk consider that if it is windy at sea level it will be blowing a gale on the peaks. You can literally get blown off your feet. Mobile phone coverage is very good on the island even in the most remote areas; it is a good idea to be equipped with one for emergencies. If walking alone it is essential to inform someone of where you are going and an estimated time of return. Amorgos may be in the Mediterranean but even islanders have died in the mountains here by falling and succumbing to hypothermia overnight. Having said all of this the aim of the game is to be sensible and not to attempt anything that maybe beyond your capabilities.

Normal walker's rules of the countryside apply of course. To be honest if you see any rubbish on the paths (usually cigarette packets) it is not the fault of visitors. It would be a service to the island if you could pick up any refuse you see; discarded refrigerators are exempt. You will find many paths that seem to be blocked by fences. If you look carefully you will find a way through that has been tied up with string or a piece of wire. Obviously please re-secure the fence after passing through.

Walking on Amorgos is always exciting as there is something different to see and varying experiences every day. The other attraction is that in a two week stay and by following this guide you can see most of the island and almost truly say, 'we have done Amorgos'. Following the walks described can be as challenging or as easy as you wish, the aim is flexibility. You are even offered the occasional optional challenge to explore on your own. Most of the places described are not visited by the great majority of visitors to the island. Every walk has been mapped out with military precision. Every 'instruction' has been tested to 'destruction'. This guide is all you need to find your way to the 'secrets' of the 'secret jewel'. GPS reference points are supplied; a GPS is not essential but is highly recommended on two occasions in this guide. To carry a compass is always a very good idea wherever you are walking. Many paths are not marked on any other maps of the island apart from in this book. Some marked paths are protected and maintained[1] these are allocated numbers. Please note that there is no connection between these

---

[1] See Acknowledgements

numbers and the walk numbers in this guide. For each walk a map is enclosed in the guide which has been prepared by cartographers Anavasi[1], but walkers may wish to also carry a map of the whole island, even if only for interest. The Anavasi topo for Amorgos is The Aegean Cyclades series No. 10.27, scale: 1:35,000.

Opposite the map of each walk are the precise directions to follow. To the left of these is the distance in metres between each instruction. The bracketed figures are GPS waypoints (WP). These are listed on a following page giving the coordinates in latitude and longitude in degrees, minutes and fractions of a minute. The maps are marked up with the WGS84 geographic coordinates system datum. GPS users should ensure that their system is set up accordingly (setup menu, units). Magnetic declination on Amorgos (2010) is 3º45'E (declination positive).

Dr David Livingstone would have appreciated a guide book such as this.

Kastri Ancient Arkesini

[1] See Appendix: useful websites

Part 2

Places of Interest and Walking Guides

Introduction

The island of Amorgos is essentially split into three areas: Aegiali to the northeast, Chora and Katapola in the centre and Kato Meria to the southwest. In ancient times each area was controlled by one of the three ancient City States with distinct marked boundaries and their own coinage. Indeed, up until recent times each area had separate local administrations with their own council and mayor. Ancient roads were established linking the three ancient cities and formed the foundation of the current paths between the villages and different parts of the whole island. Before the asphalt road was completed the islanders travelled around either by foot or donkey using these paths, the other option being to travel by caique between Aegiali and Katapola. Because of their relative isolation from each other the communities in the separate areas have developed distinct differences from each other including speaking in their own dialects.

Area of Vigla (Aegiali)

General Notes on the area

The area of Aegiali is very mountainous and consequently has the highest rainfall. There are also an abundance of natural springs that are still used today to provide water to the villages and farms. However some land in the Akrotiri area has become barren since the earthquake of 1956 caused some springs to disappear underground or change course. Today there are the three main villages of Langada, Tholaria and Potamos, and also the port. The port has only become developed in recent years. In ancient times the district was controlled by the ancient city of Vigla, which is located on a defensive promontory close to the village of Tholaria and was first occupied in the 7th century BC and abandoned in the medieval period. All that remains today are the ruins of a temple, some stone steps and the base for three statues dedicated to the goddess Hera. In this area of Aegiali it is thought that one of the major gods to be worshipped was Asclepius as farmers have dug up many ancient coins bearing his device over the centuries.

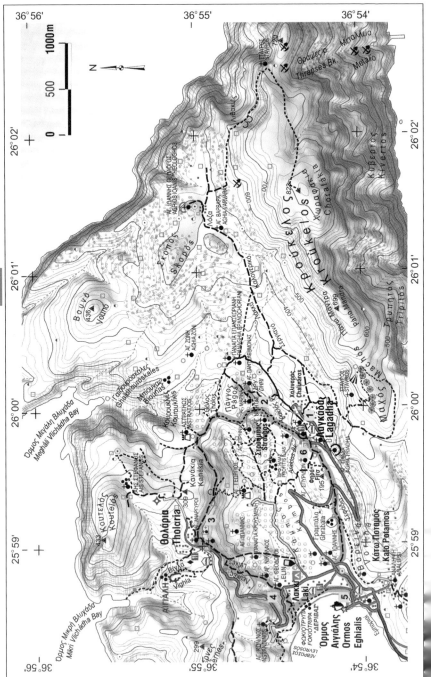

Walk 1 Stroumbos

Walk 1 Stroumbos (Options: 2.8 kms – 7.6 kms)

This is a circular walk and the instructions start and finish in Langada but it can just as easily be started in the port of Ormos or Tholaria as it passes through both of these locations. It is in three sections, the most popular being the first part from Langada to Tholaria. This is in fact a fashionable route with visitors to the island in the summer and the easiest in this guide. However, even on this walk there are hidden and special places which most people just walk past without knowing. The first section takes you through the remote village of Stroumbos and onto Tholaria with spectacular views across the bay of Aegiali below. From Tholaria you follow a well paved donkey path down to the bay past a delightful spring. From the port the route takes you back up another well paved path back to Langada. Public or private transport can be used to cut the walk short in Tholaria or down in the port.

Places of Interest

Langada

The area around the modern village of Langada was first settled on in the Cycladic period due to the attraction of the springs nearby. The present village was purposely positioned behind the large Troutsoula rock so that it was not visible from the sea and protected from attack in the days of piracy. In modern times the village has spread out and is reputed to be the longest village in Greece. The main square (Platea) is at the upper end of the village and is the centre for village festivities. Here you will find a shop, a traditional taverna and cafeneions. In the central part of the village is the main village church Agia Sophia and lower down the smaller church Agia Kyriaki. In the lower part of the village there are a selection of cafeneions, the bakery and another shop. Before local government was centralised in the capital Chora, Langada was the capital of Aegiali and was where the government offices and post office were located. In more modern times a mechanical mill was built to replace the traditional windmills located on the mountain above the village. The name of Langada is derived from the Greek word for gorge due to its location perched above the Araklos torrent-bed.

Postal Service

We went to collect our post one day and Anna, the post-mistress, was giggling laying all the letters on the road outside the post office. We thought that this was a rather bizarre practice but you get used to most things on Amorgos. When we got closer we noticed that all the letters and parcels were soaking wet. She was putting them in the sun to dry. 'What happened? Have you had a plumbing leak in the shop?' we asked. 'No,' she said, 'they were throwing the mail sacks off the ship onto the quay and this one missed and went into the sea'. The only thing for us was an annual return for Companies House in the UK. I filed a very wrinkled return with a letter of explanation and heard no further about it. I am sure that one went in their book of companies excuses.

Out of the Rat Race into the Fire

Prophet Elijah chapel

The small Prophet Elijah chapel is perched on the edge of a sheer cliff and is built on an ancient sacrificial site. Archaeological finds have been dated to the Early Cycladic period. Near the chapel is an ancient stone block which is probably a tombstone for an important official or priest not, as reported in other sources, a sacrificial altar. The sacrifices were most likely performed by throwing the sacrificed animal over the edge into the gorge below.

Araklos Gorge

The Araklos Gorge is the main torrent-bed of Aegiali and in very heavy and prolonged rain the water gushes down from the mountains and into the valley below. However most of the year it is dry and full of flowering oleanders and at the bottom orchids can be found in spring and autumn. The locals believe that a dragon lives in the gorge and on Easter Monday an effigy of Judas is thrown down there to feed it so that it is safe to go down for the rest of the year. They also believe that there is a ghost called Lola in the gorge and consequently avoid going down there in the dark.

Stroumbos

The village of Stroumbos is known as the village of '12 houses and 13 ovens' as each house had its own oven as well as there being an extra oven outside one of

Agios Nikitas, Stroumbos

Stroumbos

the houses. The extra oven was considered to bring good luck to the village and ensure that no one would go hungry. Stroumbos is believed to be on the site of the oldest settlement in Aegiali, however the current houses are only about 300 years old. Whilst being small it was nevertheless a self-contained village with a church, weaver, cobbler and olive press. After the Second World War the village was slowly abandoned as people either left the island or moved to Langada. Whilst it is not so many years since the houses were abandoned they are in such a state of ruin, with collapsed roofs, due to the owners taking their valuable juniper roof beams with them. Five houses have now been renovated; two are lived in all year round with the others only used in the summer months. To this day Stroumbos has no road, piped water or electricity. Rain is collected into water cisterns and lifted out by well buckets. Oil lamps provide light, bottled gas is delivered by donkey to run fridges and cookers. Olive wood is used on open fires or in wood burning stoves to produce heat. Small unobtrusive solar panels provide limited electricity to run small lights and recharge items such as mobile phones.

Stroumbos

The first village we halted at was Strymbo (sic), built in an almost inaccessible gorge—a wretched hamlet, but exceedingly picturesque, the inhabitants of which are much despised by their neighbours, as uncongenial, and a trifle nefarious in their practices. A proverb runs in Amoraos (sic) expressive of supreme contempt: 'It is like Strymbo with eight houses and twelve ovens.' Certainly we counted a great many ovens, but the houses were decidedly more numerous than their supercilious neighbours admit.

Bent, James Theodore. 1885. *The Cyclades or Life among the Insular*

Astratios

Astratios is located on the site of an ancient rural settlement. The small chapel is named after the Archangel (modern day Michalis) and behind the screen can be seen a 5th century BC Corinthian capital-column. Within the walls of the stone building next to the chapel can be observed large stone blocks that are the base of a Hellenistic watchtower. Overlooking the bay of Megali Glyfada this was an ideal place for defence and lookout purposes.

Tholaria

The village of Tholaria is located near to Roman arched tombs and derives its name from the Greek word for arched (tholos). The church is named after the Anargiri Saints who are supposed to possess miraculous healing powers. It is believed that the church was built on the site of a temple dedicated to Asclepius, the ancient god of healing. Many ancient stones were used in its construction and some can be seen in the walls nearby and in the gateway. Also in the area have been found Hellenistic tomb reliefs, vases, steles and archaic kouri, which originated from Naxos. Near to the church are a few traditional cafeneions and small shops. The majority of the population here still make a living from agriculture in the fields around the village.

Fokiotripa

Fokiotripa (seal hole), is a small natural bay which was used by the Romans as a natural harbour and was home to Monk seals. Further along the beach can be seen the remains of a Roman quay and Bathhouse.

Papa Costas

Ormos Aegialis

Ormos Aegialis was very small with only a few buildings and originally called Saint Nicholas after the church on the front. With the quay, road and electricity in the 1980's came increased tourism with the result that Ormos Aegialis has slowly grown into a village with pensions, shops and tavernas. Many local people still go out in their small wooden boats to fish and can sometimes be seen cleaning fish and beating ink out of an octopus on the quay. There is also a small fishing fleet with larger caiques which bring in their catch for the local people.

Agia Triada

High up in the cliffs this small chapel was built in the years of piracy and is named after the Holy Trinity. The caves inside were used to hide food and the position used as a lookout post.

Caiques at Ormos Aegiali

Walk Information

The start of this walk is at the Pagali Hotel (Nikos' Taverna) in Langada. This is the first complex in the village on the left as you drive up the road from Ormos. If you use the bus ask to be dropped off at Nikos'. If you are in the platea in Langada walk down through village for a few minutes and it is on the left just after the bakery. This whole route is very easy terrain. It starts off at 226m then after dropping down into the gorge (135m) below Stroumbos it then climbs back up again to then run almost level for some time and then a small climb up to the village of Tholaria (195m). It then descends to sea level and back up to Langada (226m). There are shops and tavernas in Langada, Tholaria and Ormos so very little water needs to be carried. There are buses to Langada, Tholaria and Ormos so this walk can be cut short by completing just one or two sectors. It can also of course be started in any of the three villages.

Distances:	Langada - Tholaria:	2.8 kms
	Tholaria - Ormos Aegialis:	2.7 kms
	Ormos Aegialis - Langada:	2.1 kms

Instructions

From Nikos' Taverna (1) in *Langada* proceed down the path through the village. Take the first turning to the right after the church. Go straight ahead passing the shop on the left and head down the path to the water cistern on the right. This is good drinking water.

300   Continue on the stone path ahead down to the bottom of the *Araklos* gorge towards the small village of Stroumbos seen ahead. At the beginning on the left across the gorge you will see the *Prophet Elijah Chapel*.

430   At the bottom of the gorge bear left up the slope to *Stroumbos* passing the church of Agios Nikitas (2) as you enter the village.

70   Pass through the village bearing left after the last house to climb up a small slope. Go straight past the turning on the right and proceed over the brow of the hill down to the spring of Thekla.

280   From the spring go straight ahead up the slope onto the path that takes you around the top of the valley towards *Tholaria*. Along this scenic route after a little way you will see on your right a ruined Roman church.

425   Continue around the path and you will see a sign on the right saying *Astratios*. This is a place many people just walk straight past without popping down to have a look.

275   Continue around the top of the valley to the bottom of the steps (3) leading up into *Tholaria*.

1,050   Proceed straight up all the steps passing to the right of the church of *Agii Anargiri*. At the top you come to the main street with a number of cafeneions.

272   Turn left down the street and left again past the church down to the car

90	Proceed straight across the car park where you will find the mule track down to Ormos. Continue straight down initially bearing right until you come to a junction.
327	Go up to the right and then down to pass the very attractive spring complex on the right. Continue down passing Agios Nikolaos on the left, through the olive groves and down to the road (4).
915	Turn left onto the road and immediately right down the path alongside the house towards the sea. Keep right at the gateway. Bear left and down to the beach at *Fokiotripa*.
318	Walk along the beach to the port of *Ormos Aegialis* (5) where there are many tavernas, bars and shops.
755	From the end of the beach turn left up hill on the road towards Langada. Go past the turning to Tholaria on the left and take the first right. Immediately on your left you will see the old mule track up to Langada.
385	Proceed straight ahead up this path crossing the main road two thirds of the way up. Towards the top, on the cliffs on the right, you will see *Agia Triada*. Continue on into lower Langada (6)
1,400	Turn right up the street to find Nikos' Taverna a little further up on the right.
285	

GPS Waypoints

No.	Latitude and Longitude (Degrees and Minutes)	Elevation (m)
1	N36° 54.352 E025° 59.843	226
2	N36° 54.603 E025° 59.940	154
3	N36° 54.991 E025° 59.202	187
4	N36° 54.516 E025° 58.680	24
5	N36° 54.094 E025° 58.651	0
6	N36° 54.310 E025° 59.677	192

Local village wedding, Agia Sophia, Langada

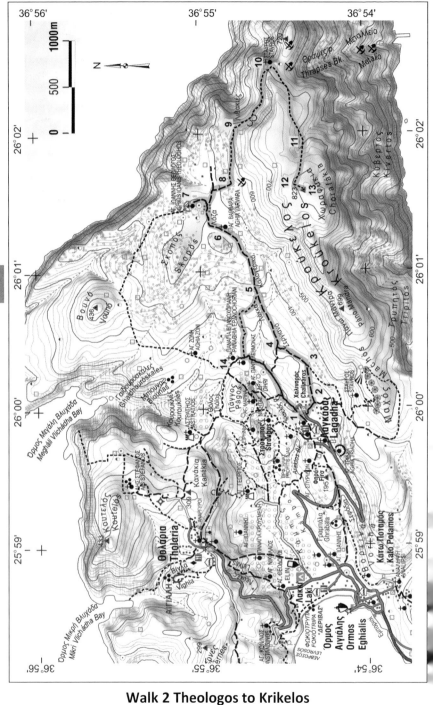

Walk 2 Theologos to Krikelos

Walk 2 Theologos - Krikelos   (Options: 6.4 kms – 13.6 kms)

This walk starts in Langada and takes you to the top of Krikelos, the highest mountain on Amorgos. It is in four distinct sections which can be accomplished progressively with turn back options at any time. A weather check is essential if you intend to proceed to the top and also GPS and/or a compass is recommended for this last section. The first target is the remote monastery of Theologos; this is a gentle climb all the way up and the path is very easy. The reward is to see this magnificent C6[th] AD church. The next section takes you to the cliffs on the way to Stavros. This is an incredible and alpinistic view with the sea 600m below you. You can then proceed to Stavros along the cliff path; this is not a section for vertigo sufferers. Stavros can be very windy but there is a shelter there. From this little church you can proceed up to the summit. The return is essentially the same way but takes you via Panagia on the way back before returning to Langada.

Places of Interest

The Krikelos Forest

The area above Langada was heavily forested with juniper, oak and cypress, and in the 1800's Aegiali was known as Melania after the Greek word for black or dark as the forest looked like a bruise or dark stain when viewed from the sea. Much wood was exported to the surrounding islands, particularly Santorini. In 1835 the forest burnt down in a fire that lasted 20 days and, due to soil erosion and grazing by goats, it never regenerated. In ancient times the shepherds in this area worshipped Pan, the god of shepherds and flocks, the shepherds using pipes to send warning signals and for playing music.

Theologos

The monastery of Saint John Theologos was built in 530AD on the site of an ancient temple dedicated to Pan. Stones from the original temple were used in its construction along with volcanic stone from Milos. By the 1990's the buildings were in a parlous state but in the past few years it has been renovated using donations from the local people, the church and also the Bishop of Athens. In one of the side rooms an ancient urn was found hidden in a niche and is thought to contain the remains of an important priest. Behind the screen the Byzantine frescoes remain untouched although the stonework around them has been repaired. The monastery is named after Saint John of the Revelation, the Greek word Theologos coming from theos 'the good or God' and logos 'the word'. The land around the monastery was farmed by the monks and by local people who rented land from the church. The walled areas nearby contained many fruit trees, of which only a few remain.

Stavros

From Stavros (Holy Cross) the summit of Krikelos (Mount Chorafakia) can be reached. A festival is held every year at Stavros on 14th September. There is a very dangerous path that leads from here to the area of Papas where a few trees can be

Tobbac Harris

Later in the year we took our clients to Theologos again. It is a remote sixth century AD monastery one hour walk from the nearest village. Inside are some incredibly well preserved frescos from the period and the monks have lovingly maintained the whole building over the centuries. It is without doubt one of the most spectacular buildings on the island and rarely visited by tourists due to its location. A little further around the mountain is a now derelict house. This is where an old goatherd and farmer Tobbac Harris used to live. When Tobbac used to live there, about fifty years ago, he was half a day's donkey ride away from the nearest cigarette supply and like most islanders had an insatiable desire for the weed. He used to overcome the problem by growing his own tobacco on the terraces. As much as he tried however he couldn't replicate cigarette paper. At, presumably, one of the twice yearly festivals at the monastery he was pondering his predicament during a very involved and protracted sermon by the priest. Idly thumbing and flicking the delicate pages of the ancient handwritten prayer book it came to him like a vision from God, it was clearly meant to be. The paper was just the perfect weight and texture to 'roll your own' and he was sure that the ornate and intricate calligraphy would not affect the taste. Frequent nightly sorties were made and supplies acquired. History does not record if the demise of Tobbac coincided with the total depletion of all the pages of all the ancient prayer books but there are certainly none to be seen today.

Out of the Rat Race into the Fire

found and are all that remains of the forest. There are also the remains of the path leading down to Metallio the Bauxite (aluminium ore) mine, which operated

Theologos

between 1929-1940. The workforce of the mine were from Langada and also other islands and were accommodated in a village next to the mine which had its own taverna and bakery. Most supplies arrived by boat but once a week the Langada baker's daughter was sent down with a mule carrying supplies, the journey from Stavros taking one hour. The ore was ground on site and then loaded onto ships. The path has now seriously deteriorated and the safest way to get there these days is by boat. Many of the buildings still remain intact with furniture and filing cabinets inside, however the mine itself is considered dangerous to enter. The seam of bauxite runs north from the mine across the island. On the more accessible northern slopes of Krikelos there is evidence of bauxite being mined there in Neolithic times. Bauxite axe heads from this period have been found in Crete. There is a theory that the source of this bauxite was Amorgos and research is currently taking place to establish this claim.

Panagia
The church of Panagia is built on the foundations of an ancient temple and contains many stones taken from other temples in the area. The festival of Panagia takes place on August 15th and, after Easter and Christmas, it is the most important festival in Greece and a national Bank holiday. This is Langada's major festival and large parties take place in the village to celebrate. There are many water holes in the area surrounding Panagia that are called embigi (blood hole). These water holes were supposed to have been formed by blood flowing from the church after pirates attacked faithful pilgrims there. Near to Panagia is the chapel of Agios Dimitrios, which has been constructed of the same stone as Theologos and has the same distinctive domed roof design. It is most likely that this miniature version of Theologos was built first to test out the design of the roof before building the monastery.

Walk Information

This four section walk starts and finishes in the platea in Langada. There is a bus stop there. If followed all the way this route takes you from Langada platea (256m) to Theologos (514m), Stavros (662m), and to the top of Krikelos (823m). The path to Theologos is excellent, complete with many stone steps and even the occasional stone bench built to sit on. From Theologos to 'Alpine Corner' (authors' designation) the path is a basic mule track. Around the cliffs onto Stavros is a narrow cliff path crossing areas of scree. This section is not for vertigo sufferers. This path should also be avoided in high winds. Stavros to the summit of Krikelos is a good mountain path, but not well marked, on barren ground. A GPS is recommended for this last section or at least a good compass should be carried. Now then you have made it to the top of our little world. However, the summit is very rounded and you can't see anything within 5km, though on a clear day you can see to the far end of the island and many of the other islands of the Cyclades. There is no water available anywhere on the whole route. You will however be returning the same way after WP5 so leaving water at way points on the way up is recommended. A stone on top of the bottle is a local sign that it is 'owned'. If proceeding beyond Theologos it is essential to obtain a weather forecast and be aware of high winds and low cloud.

Distances:	Langada - Theologos:	3.2 kms
	Langada - Alpine Corner:	4.5 kms
	Langada - Stavros:	5.3 kms
	Langada - Krikelos Peak:	6.8 kms

Instructions

In the car park at the platea proceed up the slope to the right of the bus shelter, turn left at the top and then first right. Continue up the stepped slope turning left at the top. Carry straight on and up the stone steps past the stables to the top (2).

444 Carry on along the path taking the right hand turn at the end. Follow the path up and turn left onto the plateau with water holes at the top (3).

260 With the water cistern on your right go straight ahead down the slope and continue to the junction (4).

400 Bear right and follow the path along eventually coming to the top of the *Araklos* gorge down which a river flows in the winter. Proceed up the stone steps ahead to the junction at the top (5).

550 Turn right and follow the stone steps up to the top. Proceed ahead through the shady cutting until you come out at Agia Barbara (6).

953 From this point you can see *Theologos* ahead in the distance. Proceed towards the monastery. You may have to pass through a gate (hinged fence), please close it after you. Just below the monastery turn left up the access slope up to Theologos (7).

560 For the second section on to Stavros leave the monastery walking back down the slope. Continue straight ahead at the bottom passing to the right the way you arrived. Continue ahead to the stone wall and turn left to follow it along. At the end turn right to keep following the wall as it curves around up the slope. After a while you come to a gateway (8). Through this gateway is a hidden Neolithic bauxite mine.

643 Without going through the gate turn half left to traverse the slope up marked with cairns to 'Alpine Corner' (9) at the top. In the Spring along this route there are many alpine flowers.

660 From this point the path can be seen working its way along the cliffs to *Stavros* in the distance. Follow the path to its conclusion at Stavros (10). Look out for interesting caves up to the right along this route.

823 [At Stavros there are two options for the adventurous not covered in this guide. It is possible from this point to work your way to the eastern tip of the island where there are still some trees remaining from the Krikelos forest. This is not a route for the faint hearted. It is also possible from Stavros to go down to the abandoned bauxite mine, Metallio. This is a difficult and steep route where the old path has fallen away in most places. It is a very tough walk back up and remember; there are no water supplies. The old mine taverna closed in 1940! But, it still stands.]
From Stavros to continue to the peak proceed from the church past the festival buildings on the right up the slope ahead. A little way ahead you will find crystal deposits amongst the rocks. At this point you are crossing a seam of bauxite and you will also find many rocks of this mineral. Proceed following the few cairns to the ruined farmhouse (11).

860 Bear left and head to the cairn on the ridge just ahead.

60 Turn right and head for the cairn (12) on the corner of the ridge on the skyline.

360	At the cairn turn left up to the peak.
254	From the peak retrace your footsteps. Return to the cairn (12) do not try to take a short cut, there is a cliff in the way. (If you have been stupid enough to be caught out by low cloud the bearing back to the cairn is 027° mag. From there head east until you drop down the sloping ridge and you will find a rocky slope down to your left (north). You can carefully descend this slope in the dip until you drop out of cloud and you will see the monastery of Theologos just over 1km ahead to the north. Head towards it. This is an emergency descent and should be treated as so.) From Stavros chapel (10) turn left through the gap in the wall to follow the cliff path back to 'Alpine Corner' (9). Traverse back down the slope to the gate (8) turn right and follow the wall down turning left at the bottom to follow it along. Turn right at the end back towards Theologos (7).
3,260	Turn left by the farm buildings below the monastery and retrace your footsteps past Agia Barbara (6) through the cutting and down the stone steps to the bottom (5).
1,480	At this point turn right, do not turn left which was the way you came up. Continue straight on all the way down to Panagia (14). You may have to pass through a gate (moveable fence).
520	At Panagia turn left onto the concrete path and follow it all the way back to Langada. Approaching the village go straight ahead and take the steps up through the village back into the Langada platea (1).
1,090	

GPS Waypoints

No.	Latitude and Longitude (Degrees and Minutes)	Elevation (m)
1	N36° 54.387 E025° 59.929	256
2	N36° 54.381 E026° 00.167	324
3	N36° 54.365 E026° 00.306	358
4	N36° 54.539 E026° 00.448	335
5	N36° 54.639 E026° 00.774	360
6	N36° 54.856 E026° 01.307	482
7	N36° 55.014 E026° 01.456	514
8	N36° 54.800 E026° 01.628	542
9	N36° 54.772 E026° 02.059	604
10	N36° 54.542 E026° 02.478	662
11	N36° 54.511 E026° 01.939	755
12	N36° 54.484 E026° 01.669	792
13	N36° 54.366 E026° 01.586	823
14	N36° 54.794 E026° 00.348	257

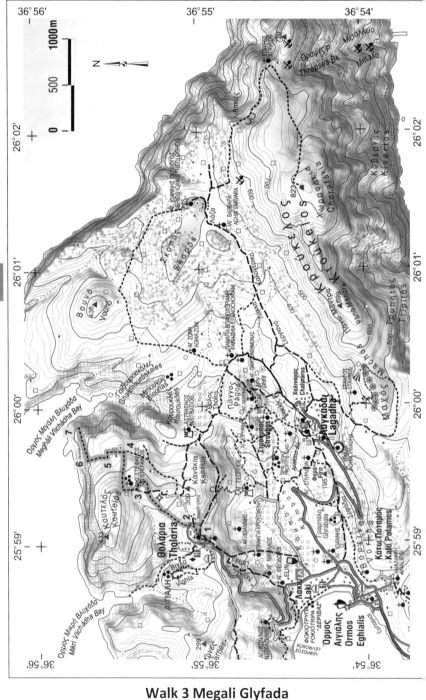

Walk 3 Megali Glyfada

Walk 3 Megali Glyfada   (5.8 kms)

Megali Glyfada is a destination many people have tried to get to but failed or got lost or, in some cases, dramatically stuck down there and had to be rescued. The route described here is the only easy way to see this spectacular bay, with the very best views on the approach. The walk starts and finishes in Tholaria and is the same way there and back. GPS is recommended but not essential. After passing a number of ruined farm houses and a cave with a spring you continue to the cliffs above the bay of Megali Glyfada – an amazing and stunning view. It is possible at this point to continue down to the beach below by an old donkey path. This descent is not covered in detail but an option for the more adventurous. From above, the beach looks glorious and tempting. Unfortunately it is northerly facing and attracts a lot of rubbish from the sea during the winter months, including tar.

> ### Goat Skin Wine Containers
> I did not like the wine they gave us at a remote spot where we lunched that day. It came out of dried goats' skins, with the hairs left on and turned inside; this gives it a strong flavour, suggestive of goats, which nearly made me sick; but it seemed to please Papa Demetrios, who drank of it freely and grew very gay. He proposed I should stay a very long time at Amorgos, and that he would take me to shoot wild goats on Mount Krytelos, that distant peak to the north of the island, far away from houses or civilisation; and when the summer came we could sleep in the open and have rare sport. But I could only give him the indefinite promise of next year, the only way of escaping from these pressing invitations of hospitality.
>
> Bent, James Theodore. 1885. *The Cyclades or Life among the Insular*

Points of Interest

The main aim of this walk from Tholaria[1] is to follow a hidden path to one of the finest views on Amorgos; very few people are acquainted with this route. It is very overgrown in places because almost no one goes this way anymore. On the walk you will see old areas of agriculture that date back centuries. Just below the farmhouse (WP5) to the left observe a tall stone circular construction. There are only a few of these remaining on the island. It is where they burnt the Greek Spiny Spurge (*Euphorbia acanthothamnos*) down to a fine ash. You see these bushes all over the island and they are prolific in this area. This white ash was mixed with water and this is what they utilised to paint the outside of the houses. It was of course easier to burn the bushes where they grew and just transport the ash.

Walk Information

Starting at the car park and bus stop in Tholaria (197m) the first part is climbing the steps through the village to the top. It then proceeds along a tractor track and then a well used old path before starting along an old mule path which is rarely used these days. From the top of the ridge (334m) outside Tholaria the route takes you

---

[1] See walk 1

down this path which is very stony and rough underfoot (boots recommended) and overgrown with thorny bushes (long trousers recommended). After passing some abandoned farm buildings the path descends steeply to a flat area with dramatic cliffs and a cave spring. To reach the target the route takes you along the contours of rough ground to a spectacular viewing point above Megali Glyfada (150m). From here there is an option to descend down to the bay. This route is only pointed out not described. There is no water en route apart from the spring but access to this water can be difficult and the purity can't be guaranteed. The walk returns the same way.

Instructions

From the car park in Tholaria (1) take the steps up into the village bearing round to the right after the church. Take the first right before the telephone and continue up the steps bearing left towards the taverna Panorama and right in front of it. Take the next main turning left and then up the steps. Keep going up the steps weaving left and right heading towards the radio masts until you come to the concrete road (2) at the top.

375 Continue up the slope following the tractor track towards the radio masts. Pass behind the mast and follow the path along until you come to a stable on your right and a large water cistern on the left (3).

950 Turn right straight after the stable through a gap in the wall and bear left across the field with the church to your right. Join the rocky path ahead and keep following it down to a junction (4).

570 Turn left towards the sea. After fighting your way through the undergrowth turn left at the end and keep straight on with the sea on your right. Turn right at the end towards the sea and drop down to the old farmhouse (5).

484 Step down over the wall and continue straight down the steep slope. Turn right at the bottom just before the wall on the corner of the cliff. At this point you will come to the cave with a spring (6).

218 Continue straight ahead with the sea to your left and through a gap in the wall, dropping down a metre. (In the corner you see a wall on the edge of the cliff if you peep over there it is a straight drop 170m down to the sea.). Keep to the left of the small wall with the sea on your left and head straight on towards the cliffs ahead. When the wall ends still continue straight on to the promontory above Megali Glyfada (7)

300 [To get down to the beach turn right and follow the mule track down keeping the bay to your left. When you get to the bottom make an exact note of the point on the cliff that you drop down onto the beach to identify it for your way back.]

From the promontory above the bay to make your way back retrace your footsteps to Tholaria. Ensure that you turn right at WP4. When you get back to the church in Tholaria turn left back down to the car park.

2,879

GPS Waypoints

No.	Latitude and Longitude (Degrees and Minutes)	Elevation (m)
1	N36⁰ 55.002 E025⁰ 59.018	197
2	N36⁰ 55.091 E025⁰ 59.184	252
3	N36⁰ 55.437 E025⁰ 59.403	334
4	N36⁰ 55.470 E025⁰ 59.684	266
5	N36⁰ 55.635 E025⁰ 59.672	235
6	N36⁰ 55.734 E025⁰ 59.672	169
7	N36⁰ 55.754 E025⁰ 59.862	150

Megali Glyfada

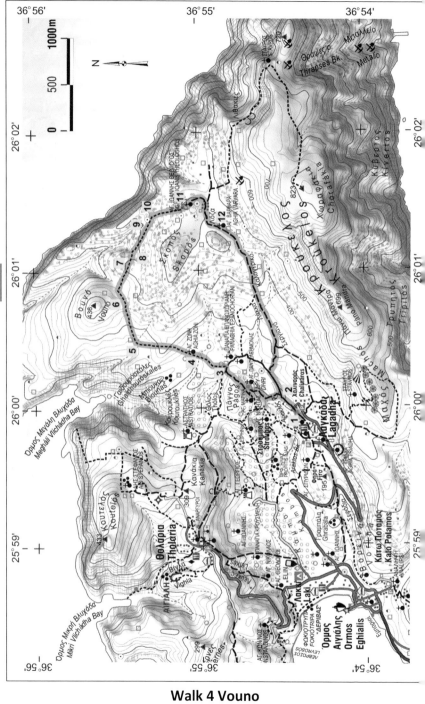

Walk 4 Vouno

Walk 4 Vouno (The Holes) - Theologos   (7.6 kms)

This is a circular walk starting and finishing in Langada with no shorter alternatives and only a turn back option if you wish to cut the tour short. This walk is for the intrepid; GPS is recommended and a compass is essential. This route takes you to a hidden area where only the goatherds (and you) tread. Even their donkeys are equipped with GPS! And, cruise control of course. This path is not marked on any map apart from the one in this book. It takes you into the mountains behind Langada to an enormous geological feature know as 'the big hole' below the peak of Vouno. This hole is almost perfectly cylindrical and an estimated 20 metres across and 150 metres deep. It is connected at the bottom by tunnels going off to other caves in the area. Around the corner there is one of these caves and there are a considerable amount of crystal deposits in the area. The walk continues towards the cliffs which plunge 400 metres straight down into the sea. Working your way from this area through old settlements you approach the Monastery of Theologos from behind. From there you descend back down to Langada.

Donkey Saddles

The saddle can be used to sit on (always side saddle facing starboard) but is also used to attach a number of accessories. There are two main types of accessory. The first is used for carrying bulky loads such as boxes. This consists of two platforms fitted one on either side of the saddle. They are like small wooden stretchers and sit almost horizontally but angled slightly inwards so the load does not slip off. They are suspended from each end top piece of the saddle and a crossing over strap stops them from swinging. The second accessory is for carrying loose loads such as grain, sand or pebbles. This is rather ingenious. Two beer crates are taken and their insides and bottoms are removed to leave just the outside shell. The bottom is cut out of a sack and it is placed inside the crate and tied around the top so that you have a hessian tube dangling out of the bottom of the crate. The bottom of the tube is then tied up to form a bag with the top kept rigid by the crate. Each crate is then tied, one to either side of the donkey. The bag is then filled with the load and it is transported to destination. When there, the bottom of the bag is untied and all the contents drop out, much to the relief of the donkey.

Out of the Rat Race into the Fire

Places of Interest

Dris and Panteleamon

In ancient times the spring of Dris was the centre for the cult of Asclepius and to this day the locals believe that the water has healing properties. Local people still use this spring to water their land nearby and for drinking. The chapel of Panteleamon is situated a short distance up the gorge and is always a cool and sheltered place. Saint Panteleamon is the saint for everyone (the Greek word pan meaning 'all' and named after the god Pan who was loved by all the other gods despite his mischief) and the festival celebrated here is for everyone especially for those people without a specific 'name day'. Because the god Pan was fun loving and playful this festival is traditionally for the children of Aegiali and afterwards they all join in with various games.

Agios Zoni

Agios Zoni (Saint Belt) is so named after the birthing belt of the Virgin Mary and thus the close proximity of this chapel to Panagia. This particular Saint has healing properties particularly for women and this probably explains the number of headscarves bearing pictures of belts offered as votives within the chapel.

The Vouno Holes

There is evidence that in this area was an important Early Cycladic settlement with the holes being used for sacrificial rituals. In more modern times locals used to collect wild honey from the sides by lowering a man into the hole on a platform secured with ropes. Geologically these holes have formed over millions of years by water dissolving the soft rock, which was encased in the hard outer rock. Salts in the rainwater crystallising in layers formed the crystal deposits nearby.

Walk Information

Starting from the platea in Langada, where there is a bus stop, the walk is circular and finishes at the same point. At any time of course you can opt to turn back the same way you came. You will be working your way along paths overgrown in places and trousers or long socks are recommended due to the thorny bushes. Walking boots are also recommended. There is no water available en route. The route is described in detail but this is a difficult one navigationally. A GPS should be used but a competent map reader ought to be able to manage with just a good compass. For a longer day out this walk can be combined with walk no. 2.

Instructions

	From the platea in Langada[1] (1) proceed east out of the village down the steps and path and take the first left (2) after the vines down into the gorge.
370	Proceed down and follow the path along the gorge to the spring of *Dris*. [If you continue along past the spring up the gorge you will find water holes and the church of *Panteleamon*.] To continue the walk follow the steep slope up to the left of the spring and turn right at the top. Continue along until you come to a junction with a water hole on the right (3).
880	Turn right and first left after climbing a few stone steps. Follow this path along keeping to the right to *Agios Zoni* (4).
570	Continue ahead bearing around to the left. [180m after Agios Zoni you will see a turning to the left which will take you to an unmarked Neolithic site. Many obsidian blades can be seen from this period in the area. Please do not touch them there may be an archaeological dig there some time in the future.] After passing this turning bear right up the hill and follow the path to a point above Megali Glyfada (5).
640	Bear right up the hill on a heading of 050⁰ passing a farm house and eventually coming to a rocky promontory ahead (6).

[1] See Walk 1

400	Bear right heading 080⁰ up the slope passing to the right of the promontory. At the top of the slope go through the farm buildings to parallel the overgrown path. You are aiming for the saddle of the ridge straight ahead bearing 100⁰. Continue on this track to the top of the ridge. Turn right at the tall stone wall and go ahead bearing 145⁰. Passing the stable on your right keep straight ahead through the ruined farm buildings following the rock formation around to the left. The *Vouno Hole* is bearing 040⁰ through rough bush (7). Take great care at the edge of the hole, the ground is falling away. It is a long way down.
520	[If you continue around to the right of the hole by scrambling over rocks and through bushes you will find a cave entrance which slopes down towards the big hole. Just below this you will find the many crystal deposits]. From the big hole you are heading towards the farm buildings bearing 100⁰. To pick up the path go away from the hole and aim for the wall ahead. Proceed through the farm complex (8).
220	Continue on the heading of 100⁰ up the slope picking up the shepherd's trail. At the top is a stable (9).
260	Bear left to the farm buildings and goat pens. Enter the pen from the corner where the fencing meets the wall. Please refasten the gate securely. Follow the wall along to the corner by the farmhouse (10).
160	Turn right to follow the wall up. The bearing from here to Theologos is 165⁰. In places the path is overgrown and you have to parallel it. Where it ends go up onto the terracing and continue up heading 165⁰. You will see shepherd's paths meandering along. Just meander with them, all the way to Theologos[2] (11).
590	From the monastery go down the slope past the farm building and turn first right. Continue straight along the path to Agia Barbara (12).
520	From this church just follow the path all the way down towards Langada which can be seen in the distance after passing through the shady cuttings. At the bottom of the stone path just short of the village turn left onto the concrete path, follow it to the steps up to the Langada platea (1).

2,470

GPS Waypoints

No.	Latitude and Longitude (Degrees and Minutes)	Elevation (m)
1	N36⁰ 54.347 E025⁰ 59.929	256
2	N36⁰ 54.509 E026⁰ 00.077	215
3	N36⁰ 54.836 E026⁰ 00.260	238
4	N36⁰ 55.069 E026⁰ 00.382	226
5	N36⁰ 55.327 E026⁰ 00.504	276
6	N36⁰ 55.419 E026⁰ 00.736	356
7	N36⁰ 55.396 E026⁰ 01.053	407
8	N36⁰ 55.369 E026⁰ 01.172	396
9	N36⁰ 55.297 E026⁰ 01.306	446
10	N36⁰ 55.270 E026⁰ 01.395	450
11	N36⁰ 54.013 E026⁰ 01.455	519
12	N36⁰ 54.864 E026⁰ 01.307	486

[2] See Walk 2

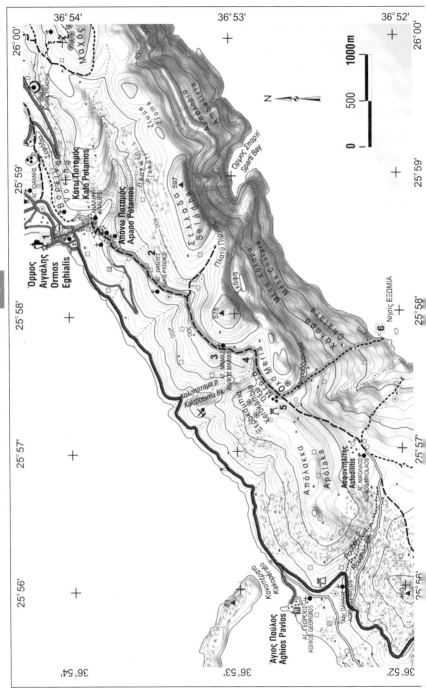

Walk 5 Halara

Walk 5 Halara (11.1 kms)

Halara is one of the very few coves on the south coast that is accessible from the land. The walk is a linear route, starting and finishing in Ormos Aegialis. The return leg is a reversal of the outbound route. It initially takes you along the main ridge path of Amorgos covered on Walk 6 and then drops down to the other side of the island past old farm properties and agricultural land. The cove is very secluded with clear deep blue water and many sea caves. Access to the water is from flat rocks or from an ancient small abandoned natural harbour. It is one of the greatest snorkelling areas on the island.

Fishing

There is a very good fish restaurant on the island, down in the harbour. This restaurant never used to rely on the fluctuations of the local fish supplies as the father used to do the fishing and the son looked after the restaurant. Some years ago we saw father out fishing. He had a very small classical wooden fishing boat that seemed as if it could only just accommodate the nets but when he had his haul on board it was really piled high and decidedly unstable. How it stayed afloat clearly defied the laws of science. The only place he could sit to row back to the harbour was on top of the whole caboodle. One evening he was still out until quite late and there was some concern about the situation at the restaurant. Not necessarily for the welfare of father but for the lack of supplies for the evening trade. The son was duly dispatched in a borrowed motorboat. When found, there was no time to transfer the load - it was just a question of a salvage operation. Father was hooked up to the back of the motorboat and towed at high speed towards the starving customers. His little wooden boat had never gone so fast in its life; the bow was well out of the water and the stern just one inch above. Father hung on for grim death perched on top of the mound of nets and fish. We didn't see him for some time after that.

Out of the Rat Race into the Fire

Places of Interest

Potamos
The village of Potamos is separated into Kato (lower) and Pano (upper) Potamos and overlooks the main gorge that runs down to Ormos Aegialis. The name comes from the Greek word for river (potamos) and in prolonged heavy rain a river runs down the gorge to Ormos Aegialis and into the sea. During the 1980's the population became very much reduced as villagers moved to Ormos Aegialis to develop pensions and shops. In more recent times, due to the construction of a road to the village, a new taverna has opened and more rooms and a pension are available for visitors, bringing new life to the village.

Nikouria
The island of Nikouria is geologically different to Amorgos, being related to the islands of Naxos, Paros and Donoussa. The peak of the island is 346 metres high and is called Halara (not to be confused with your destination). There are three beaches and in the summer small boats take people across from Agios Pavlos. In

the third century BC the island was inhabited, with fortifications, a sanctuary and a mint producing the coinage for the three city-states. In more modern times up until the late 19th century, Nikouria was used as a leper colony; the remains of the houses still being visible from the mainland. The chapel on Nikouria is called Panagia and behind it can be seen the ruins of the accommodation used by the monks who looked after the lepers. Supplies for the monks and lepers were transported by boat from the spit of Agios Pavlos to the edge of Nikouria and thrown across to the people. Today the island still belongs to the monastery and is used by the islanders as common grazing for their goats.

Agios Pavlos

The area around Agios Pavlos was settled in the Early Cycladic period and nearby can be found the remains of tombs, an acropolis, fortifications, buildings, large cut stones and two defensive towers. In more modern times the community has made a living out of agriculture and fishing.

Agios Mamas

This small chapel is built on an ancient site where artefacts from the Cycladic period have been found. It is located near to a spring, which is believed to have magical properties due to two Ley lines crossing it. The water is fed by the spring into a stone-built Venetian subterranean *cistern*.

Exo Meria

The buildings of the village Exo Meria can still be seen largely intact although it was abandoned in the early 1900's when the inhabitants either left the island or moved to Aegiali. Today one house to the edge of the main path is still lived in and the area farmed mainly with sheep, goats, cattle and poultry. As you descend towards Halara on the left can be seen the remains of a round Hellenistic watchtower.

Halara

Up until recent times Halara was a large agricultural area as can be seen by the number of farmhouses and terracing, some of which is still used for grazing. Small fishing boats were kept in the small sheltered natural harbour where the quay can still be seen. The sea is very deep and blue . Near the quay is a pool with an archway underwater into the sea. Just around the corner from this arch is an underwater cave with a blow hole above. When there is a swell the water jets out of this hole and a rainbow is formed. Halara is supposed to be a place of high energy as two Ley lines cross at this point; unfortunately you need the energy at Exo Meria once you have climbed back up!

Islets

Close to the coast at Halara and the Monastery of Hozoviotissa are two islets; Exomia and Viokastro. The legend surrounding these islets is that a pirate captain was sailing from Agia Anna below the monastery to Halara. To stop him attacking, the icon of the monastery petrified him and his ships into stone and these are the two rocks. One guide book for Amorgos which has been translated from Greek claims that they are two 'stoned pirates'!

Fresh Fish

The Limani restaurant is a beautiful setting with the tables set out underneath the stars and flowering trees where, surrounded by pots full of geraniums, you can watch the world go by. We have been sitting outside having dinner there on many occasions when a box of flapping fish has been thrown at our feet whilst the fisherman goes inside to negotiate a price. On one occasion one of the old boys, Nikitas, came along the street pulling a fish which was about five feet long and three feet across; it was certainly the biggest fish apart from sharks we had ever seen in the area. He only has a small boat and it would have been impossible for him to have landed this in his vessel; he must have towed it behind which was quite an achievement given his age and the fact that he doesn't even have an engine on his boat. He had a grin from ear to ear and was revelling in all the glory poured upon him by his rapidly growing entourage of colleagues. His boat was actually only a few yards away but he had purposely dragged it with great effort through the whole length of the village to parade his prize. He couldn't have looked more proud if he'd been walking through with a blonde international model on his arm. He stopped outside the grocery shop right by where we were sitting. Agiris came up the three steps from his shop, which is set below street level, to also admire the catch. It was all very well catching something this big but the problem then was what to do with it. It would take a month to turn it into fish cakes and there was no fridge on the island big enough to keep it. It was reluctantly agreed that the only thing to do was to cut the prize in half on Agiris' doorstep. A large knife was produced and the operation began. A few people at nearby tables went a little pale and left but we watched with interest. After 10 minutes it was clear that they were getting nowhere so a large cleaver was produced from the restaurant. As they hacked away at it chunks of fish were flying all over the place, all our clothes had to be washed that evening and Henri is still finding bits in her handbag to this day. All the time they were working on the fish it was moving about on the path; it was a real slippery critter. In their enthusiasm they hadn't noticed that it was getting closer and closer to Agiris' doorway and on the final blow which separated the top half from the bottom the whole tail shot down the steps into the shop and across the floor. It was only stopped from playing a very expensive game of skittles with all the liquor bottles by a strategically placed fridge. The fisherman was now left with the top half of the fish but no tail to tow it with, quite a quandary. A large bin bag was produced and the remaining fish was slid into it. He slung it over his shoulder and had hardly taken one pace before the weight became too much for the bag and the contents shot out of the bottom across the pavement and straight down the steps into the shop to join its other half. Everyone chased it down there and a few minutes later it was transported out in stronger sack. The old fisherman hobbled away down the street supporting the bag over his shoulder with one hand and a stick in the other, disappearing, literally, into the sunset.

Out of the Rat Race into the Fire

Walk Information

Starting in the port in Ormos, where the bus stops, this route starts off up the road to Potamos. It then proceeds up the steps through lower and upper Potamos to join the mule track at the top which is the first part of the main route along the island. It is rocky underfoot in places and on the way down from the ridge to Halara the path is sometimes rough and overgrown. Walking boots are recommended. This path down to the sea is another route that is not marked on any other maps apart from in this guide. There is no water available en route. The route takes you back the same way. Starting at sea level it rises at the highest point to 385m to then descend to Halara. This walk can be combined with walk 6.

Instructions

In the port of Ormos Aegialis (1) walk along the front of the shops and turn left just before the shipping office up the steps and the steep slope to *Potamos*. On reaching the village climb the steps to the church and turn right to keep following the steps up. At the top of this section turn a sharp left. Take the first main turning to the right and keep going up and ahead. After walking across a veranda turn left at the end up the steps. At the telephone booth turn right up the steps and keep going up through the village until you join the mule track. Continue along this to the large village water cistern (2).

1,300 Continue straight ahead and follow the path up around the contours of the mountains, with views down towards *Agios Pavlos* and the island of *Nikouria*, to the highest point on this walk *Agios Mamas* (3).

1,350 Follow the path down and around to the house (4) on the left above the spring. [To visit the spring you can go down the path straight in front of the house curving around to the left to the Venetian water cistern. To rejoin the main path continue on and back up on the other side of the valley].

243 Keep following the path through Exo Meria past the farm on your left. [To visit the old village houses and windmill turn right at this point]. From the farm continue ahead to the turning (5) left down to Halara.

1,017 Just keep following the path down past all the old farm buildings. The only slight confusion is after the last house on the right when you get into a boulder strewn area with many tall bushes. First you see a small cave on your right. The path continues over the boulder ridge straight ahead. A little further down you come across a huge rock, bear left around it and over the boulders ahead to break out of the bushy area. You will see the bay of Halara down to your left. Pick up the track going to your left and follow it to the sea as it weaves its way down (6).

1,600 Return the same way. When descending down through Potamos do not be concerned about exactly which way you came up. Just keep going down and you can't go wrong.

5,510

GPS Waypoints

No.	Latitude and Longitude (Degrees and Minutes)	Elevation (m)
1	N36° 54.098 E025° 58.629	0
2	N36° 53.535 E026° 58.333	221
3	N36° 53.109 E026° 57.749	385
4	N36° 52.995 E026° 57.717	358
5	N36° 52.667 E026° 57.347	325
6	N36° 52.111 E026° 57.740	0

Autumn flowers (Colchicum cupanni)

Katapola

Area of Minoa (Chora, Katapola)

General Notes on the Area

Situated in the central part of the island are the two main modern settlements of the capital Chora and the island's main port Katapola. The terraced mountainsides are still farmed by the locals and in the valley leading towards Katapola there are many springs. Near to Chora is an area called Terlaki, which was a settlement in ancient times, and the remains of an Hellenistic watchtower can still be seen. This area in ancient times was controlled by the ancient city of Minoa situated on a hill above Katapola called Mondoulia. Minoa was first settled on in the Neolithic era and was finally abandoned in the medieval era when Chora was developed and Katapola expanded. Within sight of Minoa remain the small settlements of Lefkes and Thekla that were built in protective positions so that signals could be seen in an emergency. The capital of Amorgos, Chora was built high up out of view from the sea and around a protective rock. Although Chora has always been the capital it is only in recent years that all local government and administration has been centralised there. Over the centuries Chora has gradually expanded with different areas being distinctive in architectural styles. It is claimed that the people purposely build Chora as a labyrinth in order to confuse any attackers and get them lost. The port of Katapola was established as an anchorage in Neolithic times and due to its very sheltered position is the main port of the island. Over the centuries Katapola has slowly expanded, firstly as a pirate base and then due to people moving from other parts of the island especially Kato Meria.

An autumn lamb

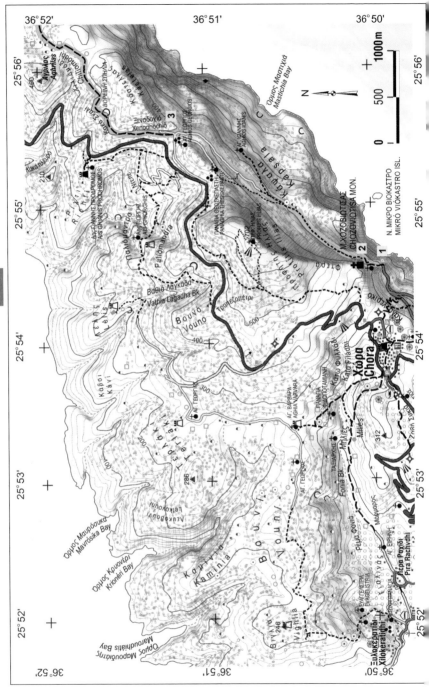

Walk 6 Part 1 Hozoviotissa to Aegiali

Walk 6 (The Ridge) Hozoviotissa - Aegiali (11.7 kms)

The ridge path from Chora[1] and the Monastery[2] of Hozoviotissa to Aegiali was the main route from one end of the island to the other from the 5th century BC and constantly in use until the completion of the road in 1998. It is a popular route with keen walkers and well documented in walking books for the Cyclades. It is a preserved and well maintained route. The walk described starts at the monastery and finishes in Ormos Aegialis[3].

Places of Interest

The Monastery of Hozoviotissa
A group of monks established the Monastery of Hozoviotissa during the 9th century AD having managed to escape from iconoclasts in Chozovo, Palestine with their precious icon of the Virgin Mary. On route from Cyprus to Constantinople they were passing the south coast of Amorgos and were struck by the similarity of the coastline to Chozovo (there is a photograph of the monastery in Chozovo in the hospitality room of the monastery and you can see the resemblance). With funding from the Patriarch and help from the local people a chapel was built high up in the cliffs. This was an area that the islanders avoided as it was supposed to be frequented by demons. Due to numerous pirate attacks this building was eventually abandoned and fell into ruins. In 1088 the Emperor of Byzantium, Alexios Komninos gave instructions for a monastery to be built on the site of the original chapel and to be given the same name.

Monastery

The position of this convent is truly awful. From the balconies one looks deep down into the sea, and overhead towers the red rock, blackened for some distance by the smoke of the convent fires; here and there are dotted holes in the rock where hermits used to dwell in almost inaccessible eyries. It is, geographically speaking, the natural frontier of Greece. Not twenty miles off we could see from the balcony the Turkish islands, and beyond them the coast of Asia Minor. In fact the Turkish island of Astypaleea seems scarcely five miles away. The Greeks say it ought to belong to them, but when the boundary line was drawn by the representatives of the Powers in conference, they had such a bad map before them that it was assigned to Turkey. Our friendly monks looked too sleepy and wanting in energy to think of suicide, otherwise every advantage would here be within their reach.

Bent, James Theodore. 1885. *The Cyclades or Life among the Insular*

---

[1] See Walk 7
[2] See Appendix: 'Etiquette' for dress code
[3] See Walk 1

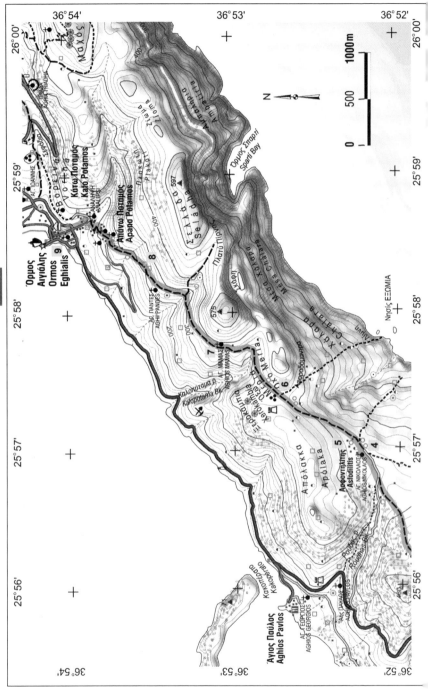

Walk 6 Part 2 Hozoviotissa to Aegiali

60

Located 300 metres above the shore, the monastery is 5 metres wide and the eight floors contain monk's cells, water cisterns, ovens, kitchens, olive and wine presses, larders, a dining room, ecclesiastical treasury and church. Entry was originally by a drawbridge that was replaced by the current steps in the 1800's. Due to its location, in the days of piracy the monastery was used as an observation post and fortress. Renovated lintels show that the monastery has been well maintained over the centuries and indeed work is still done every year to keep the building in good order. In 1833 a serious crack appeared on the outside wall and on the instructions of King Otto the two large buttresses were constructed. Unfortunately in 1892 another crack appeared between the two buttresses; King George of Greece intervened and the third almost invisible buttress was built (known as the Royal buttress). During the 1930's more repairs and maintenance were carried out including re-plastering the outside walls; this was made more of a challenge due to a shortage of funds and therefore no scaffolding. The builders were lowered down the walls in packing cases tied with ropes connected to a pulley. Rock falls have always been a hazard; James Theodore Bent in 1885 reported that a rock had recently fallen into the apse of the church and destroyed the portrait of Alexios Komninos. The last serious incident was on New Year's Eve 1975 when a huge rock fell onto the terrace and crashed through three floors. The only 'casualty' was a terrified monk as the rock narrowly missed him as it hurtled through his cell. Another rock fall revealed one of the two 'hidden' cells that were supposed to contain treasure and the boat the icon arrived in; there was much disappointment when it was found to be empty! Despite many serious rock falls there is no record of any deaths and the monks believe it is because the Virgin Mary protects people from injury.

The monastery was originally affiliated to the monastery on Patmos; the Abbot of Hozoviotissa came from Patmos and an Amogiote was Abbot of Patmos. However, in 1619 some monks travelling to Patmos were almost shipwrecked in a storm and it was decided to sever contact between the two monasteries, as travel was too hazardous. There were up to 30 monks in residence but in recent years the number has dropped to only four.

Until the mid 20th century the monastery was one of the richest in Greece and today is very famous, with many Greeks visiting it on pilgrimage. In 1952 the State expropriated a large part of the monastery's property and gave it to the islanders (some of whom donated it back). However, the monastery still remains wealthy and able to make contributions to the community and towards Church projects. Despite many treasures being stolen during the 19th and 20th centuries, the monastery still possesses many rare and valuable pieces of art. Many precious icons have been removed from isolated chapels and they are now kept for safety in the monastery. Large numbers of items are on display in the Church and in the high season the museum is open to visitors. Also on display in the Church in a glass case is the builder's chisel that forms part of the foundation myth of the monastery; when it fell out of the cliff in 1952 it was said to be a bad omen and as it turned out it was not a good year for the Church as mentioned above.

The monastery is open every day to visitors from 8am to 1pm and then 5pm to 7pm. Visitors must be correctly dressed to enter.

Agia Anna
The bay of Agia Anna is situated below the Monastery of Hozoviotissa and is famous due to being one of the locations used during the filming of Luc Besson's cult movie 'The Big Blue'. Its connection to the monastery is due to the foundation myth describing the icon of the Virgin Mary landing on this beach in a small boat of its own accord. During the summer this is a popular beach especially for people staying in Chora.

Richti
The most prominent feature at Richti is the ruined circular Hellenistic watchtower. This tower would have been used for defence as well as for lookout and warning purposes. Torches and fires would have been used to send signals to the surrounding areas in the event of an attack and the people would have fled into the mountains.

Asphondilitis
This large farming area is still cultivated and used for grazing animals despite the village itself having been abandoned. In 2007 a road up to the village was completed, which was strongly opposed by many people concerned about the preservation of the island[1]. Some of the houses are now being renovated. Before the main road was constructed between Aegiali and Chora this village was used as a halfway stopping point for people travelling along the path. Food, water and accommodation were all available. The large number of water cisterns are still

---

Buying Property
We were discussing the problems of buying property on the island with a friend. He said that it is not unknown to buy property and land, only to find that it comes inclusive with a donkey and the small print states that said animal has to be looked after for the rest of its days. The property we were considering has no land as such and only five rooms so we said that we didn't need to worry about this aspect too much. Unfortunately there was more. A friend of his bought a small house in the next village and after all the contracts were exchanged, hands shook and much rejoicing all round they moved in. The first evening they were there the front door opened and a little old lady walked in, proceeded straight past them and into their bedroom closing the door behind her. It transpired that they had not bought all the rooms in the house. This particular room belonged to an aunt who had refused to move so, unnoticed by their lawyer, that room was left out of the contract and she came along with the furniture and fittings. It cost considerably more capital and much legal wrangling before they could persuade her to leave and have the whole house to themselves.

Out of the Rat Race into the Fire

---

[1] See Appendix: Eco-Tourism

used to provide water for the farms and have recently been renovated. The carved pictures in this area date back to about 100 years ago and were made by a disabled child who was inspired by the energy of this barren and lonely place.

Walk Information

The walk starts from the car park at the monastery above the bay of *Agia Anna*. The bus stop is just a little way up the road. Buses to the monastery are infrequent in low season. It is, however, easy to get there from Chora. From the car park by the radio masts at the top of Chora there is a path down to the monastery which ends just by the bus stop. It is about a twenty minute walk down.

Although the route is well maintained it is very rocky underfoot in places and walking boots are highly recommended. Plenty of water should be carried. Plan on there being no places to collect water en route. Starting at 158m the walk rises to the highest point abeam Richti (460m) descending through Asphondilitis (290m) and then climbing to Agios Mamas (385m) followed by the descent to sea level in Aegiali.

Instructions

From the car park (1) at the monastery gates walk up the 267 steps to the entrance (2).

311   The path to Aegiali starts through the gate up the steps straight opposite the monastery door. Follow this path as it curves around the mountain side and eventually joins a cart track. Follow this straight ahead until you come to a point where many tracks join, the main road can be seen just below (3).

2,549   Go slightly right and ahead along the well marked path. Do not turn right onto the cart track up the slope. Follow the path towards the island of Nikouria[1] paralleling the main road below. This path is very apparent for the whole route. After about 800m just across the main road on the left you will observe the watch tower at *Richti*. As you approach the village of *Asphondilitis* you see the church ahead (4).

3,610   Pass through the hamlet until you come to the village water cisterns at the far end (5)

230   Bear left up the slope and continue along the path to the turning down to Halara[2] (6) on the right.

1,100   Continue straight ahead through Exo Meria[3] past the farm on your right and on towards Agios Mamas[4] (7).

---

[1] See Walk 5   [3] See Walk 5
[2] See Walk 5   [4] See Walk 5

1,260	From here just continue straight down to your destination which can be seen ahead. The next signs of civilisation are the water cisterns at the top of Potamos[1] (8).
1,350	Continue down through the village to the church. Do not worry too much about which turnings you take in the village. As long as you keep going down you can't go wrong. At the bottom of the steps below the church follow the road straight down to the port (9).
1,300	

GPS Waypoints

No.	Latitude and Longitude (Degrees and Minutes)	Elevation (m)
1	N36° 49.930 E025° 54.553	158
2	N36° 50.088 E025° 54.572	241
3	N36° 51.168 E025° 55.529	379
4	N36° 52.205 E025° 56.959	291
5	N36° 52.252 E025° 57.056	263
6	N36° 52.667 E026° 57.347	325
7	N36° 53.109 E026° 57.749	385
8	N36° 53.535 E026° 58.333	221
9	N36° 54.098 E025° 58.629	0

Sunset over Nikouria

[1] See Walk 5

Ancient terracing below Vigla Aegiali

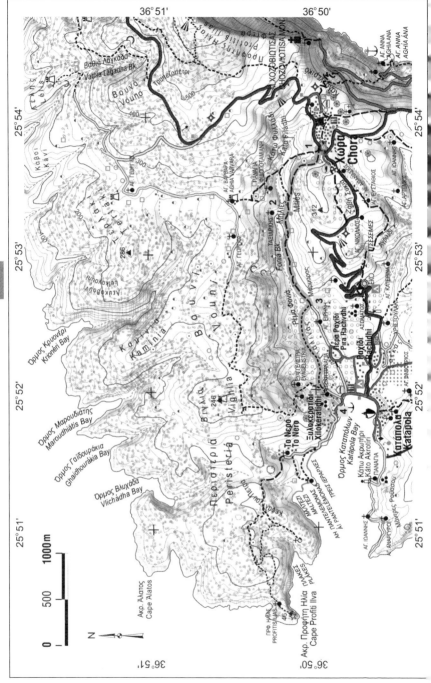

Walk 7 Chora to Katapola

Walk 7 Chora to Katapola (3.5 kms)

This is a delightful and easy walk starting in Chora descending on a preserved and well maintained path, downhill all the way. It passes through a fertile area with many springs complete with frogs and all extremely colourful in the spring. Towards the end this guide takes you away from the main path through olive groves and an orchid field bringing you out in Katapola in Xilokeratidi on the opposite side of the bay to the port.

Places of Interest

Chora
The Capital of the island, Chora, was first inhabited in the 9th century AD with the nucleus located in the area surrounding the Kastro rock. During the Venetian period fortified houses were built around the Kastro, which are supposed to have secret passages leading to the castle. The view from the chapel is very spectacular but care should be taken if it's windy. The path leading up to the Kastro consists of 5th century BC dressed stones, which probably came from a nearby temple. Over the centuries Chora has spread out and they say it was purposely built as a labyrinth to confuse the pirates and to get them hopelessly lost. Being the Capital, Chora is the administrative centre of the island and is also where the main medical centre and helipad are located. There is a large selection of cafeneions, tavernas and shops, particularly along the central street. It is well worth exploring the small streets around.

The Archaeological Collection
The archaeological collection, half way up the main street, is housed in a Venetian building that in the 18th century was owned by the wealthy Gavras family who were merchants. In 1968 the building was donated to the people of Chora when the last member of the Gavras family died (apparently a curse was placed on the family wishing them all to die childless, which is apparently what happened). Using donations from the community the building was renovated between 1972 and 1978. The collection on display consists of artefacts found on the island that date from 3000BC to the Early Christian period. Many of these items originated from the collection of Emmanuel Ioannides[1], which he donated to the citizens of Amorgos. The larger part of the whole collection is stored in two houses, the items on display to the public being carefully selected examples.

Entry to the collection is free and it is normally open in the summer months Tuesday-Sunday (except bank holidays) from 8.30am to 3pm.

Zoodochos Pygi
Next to the archaeological collection is the Byzantine church of Zoodochos Pygi (Life giving Source), which has a carved marble plaque taken from a sarcophagus

---

[1] See Walk 10 - Lefkas

laid into the floor. Dated 1683 it has a carving of the two-headed eagle and unusually bears the skull and crossbones.

Kato Lakkos
On the edge of the Medieval quarter is situated an underground water cistern that the Venetians changed to an aqueduct with archways supporting the roof. Up until modern times this was the main water supply for this part of Chora and also for the now ruined olive press next to it.

Olive Pressing
The town of Amorgos itself does not present many interesting features for the archaeologist; the churches are bare, and the houses have but rude attempts at decoration, but most of them contain many interesting relics of the Venetian days, oak chests, embroideries and pottery. There are, too, a considerable number of olive-presses here, primitive in construction, for the modern improvements which have penetrated into other parts of olive-growing Greece have not reached here yet. They consist of flat stones with a circular rim; on to this the olives are put in bags and pressed with another stone until the oil runs out into the rim, and from thence into a receptacle placed for it. Two men usually turn the upper stone by means of wooden screws and iron bars, though sometimes mules are employed for this purpose. I fancy that the olive-presses now in use in Amorgos are not very different from those which their forefathers used centuries before our era.

Bent, James Theodore. 1885. *The Cyclades or Life among the Insular*

Katapola
The port of Katapola is the main port for the island due to its sheltered location. Established in the Bronze Age it was originally the anchorage for ancient Minoa, expanding during the Hellenistic and Roman periods as it became more important for trade. The modern name comes from the Greek for 'lower city' (Kato Polis) as a consequence of its position geographically and socially to Minoa above. Katapola is essentially split into three areas; the modern port, Rachidi in the valley and Xilokeratidi on the far side. The ravine leading into the valley is called Fonias (killer) and due to the presence of many springs remains an agricultural area with olive groves and market gardens.

Katapola

The port of Katapola

During the Ottoman occupation Katapola expanded due to increased trade and pirates making it one of their main bases. Despite the government's attempts to eradicate piracy with severe punishment of those caught aiding and abetting the pirates, the islanders found it easier and more beneficial to help them and risk the consequences. By 1826 one of the most feared pirates was based on Amorgos with two ships and 35 followers. One night a band of Greek soldiers landed on the island and captured him along with 8 men and took them to Syros where they were executed. By the early 20th century, although piracy had been eradicated, the local caique captains turned to smuggling which was not only considered a lucrative sport but also benefited the population by providing essential supplies.

Up until very recent times boat yards in Xilokeratidi built caiques and small fishing boats. Nowadays they are brought from Naxos or the mainland. During the Persian Wars Amorgos, as a member of the Athenian League, fought in the Battle of Salamis (480BC) with her own ship, which was probably built in Xilokeratidi. Many ancient finds in this area include buildings and arched tombs (which have been dated to the Mycenean period but are probably actually from a later period) indicating activity here since the establishment of an anchorage by the people of Minoa.

The main port area has many shops and tavernas as well as the only bank on the island. Near the central platea is a Venetian faucet that was originally an ancient aqueduct leading from a spring on Mondoulia[1]. There are many churches that contain ancient stones in their walls, probably originating from Minoa. This area is now a very popular place for visiting yachts.

---

[1] See Walk 10

Walk Information

The walk starts from close to where the bus stops in the lower platea in Chora. Starting at 300m it descends all the way down to the sea. It is a very good path. Walking boots are not really required. A small amount of water should be carried. There are tavernas at the start and finish. The bus from Katapola at the end of the walk leaves from the port. For a longer hike this can be combined with walk 6 by starting in Katapola and walking up to Chora and then picking up the route along the ridge to Aegiali from the monastery.

Instructions

Take the steps down from the platea to the right of the statues, go through the car park and turn right along the road towards Aegiali away from the roundabout. The path is a few metres along to your left (1). Follow it along as it passes just below the heliport and keep following the contours of the valley down this well defined path. After a while you come to some springs (2)

1,090   Continue on down until you come to a road (3) with two houses to the right

1,190   Turn right down the path that runs alongside the lower house. Follow this until you come to a cart track along the river bed, turn left along this and keep following it along keeping to the left. After passing the chicken houses on the left go down the slight dip until you come to a 'T' junction. Turn right and then first left (look out in the spring for orchids in the fields to your right) and follow the path to the St George hotel. After passing the hotel follow the steps down to the sea at *Xilokeratidi* (4) on the opposite side of the port of *Katapola*.

1,210

GPS Waypoints

No.	Latitude and Longitude (Degrees and Minutes)	Elevation (m)
1	N36° 49.948 E025° 53.781	301
2	N36° 50.144 E025° 53.301	159
3	N36° 50.024 E025° 52.613	62
4	N36° 49.837 E025° 51.920	0

Training Limonia with her mother

71

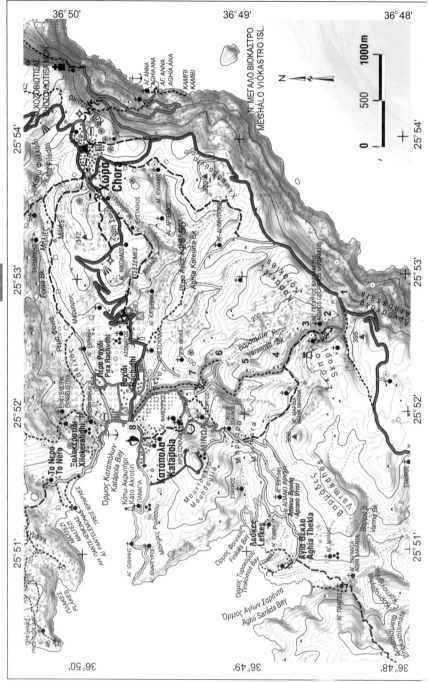

Walk 8 Agios Valsamitis to Katapola

Walk 8 Agios Valsamitis - Katapola (3.8 kms)

The path from the monastery to Katapola[1] is downhill all the way. It is a very short walk starting at this fascinating ancient monastery and following the fertile valley down to the sea. There are fantastic views across the bay on the way down. In the spring you can hear the water running down the river gorge below. This easy path is well maintained. For the more adventurous there is a very intrepid route described which takes you down the gorge.

Places of Interest

Agios Valsamitis

The Post Byzantine monastery of Agios Valsamitis was built on the site of an earlier church dating from the 9th century AD. The foundation myth surrounding this location is that lepers from a pirate ship whilst escaping from Chora[2], came upon a spring with mint growing nearby. They settled there and after a while their leprosy disappeared. News of this spread. Reinforced by an icon of Saint George being found amongst the mint, a church was built there dedicated to Saint George. Romantic stories aside, the spring was in pre-Christian times famous for its healing and prophetic properties and the site of a sanctuary.

Having fallen into ruin it was rebuilt in 1688 and again in 1796. By 1885 when James Theodore Bent[3] visited the monastery it had become a place for many to visit in order to consult the oracle. Men and women visited before marriage and sailors before a long voyage; unfortunately pirates managed to bribe the priests, and many mariners were sent unwittingly to their doom as a result. The sacred water runs into a bowl within the church and the priests would read a person's destiny by examining a glass of water using unwritten rules passed down verbally. By the 20th century a disapproving Bishop had suppressed this practice and so today visitors can drink a cup of the healing water but without their destiny being predicted! The last associated miracle connected with the monastery dates to the late 1960's; a crew member of a ship passing Amorgos dreamt that Saint George told him that there was a hole in the ship. When the dream recurred he woke the crew and they found that the ship did indeed have a hole in the hull, they managed to repair it and saved the ship from sinking. Afterwards the crew member made a pilgrimage to the monastery to offer his thanks. In the past the water level in the bowl at Easter was used to predict whether it would be a good or bad year for the farmers; if it was empty it would be a bad year and full a good year. Modern day logic tells us that the level of rainfall over the winter months determines the water level in the bowl and consequently how much water the land receives.

---

[1] See Walk 7
[2] See Walk 7
[3] See History

Unfortunately the monastery is not normally open to the public but if the gardener is there you may be allowed to enter if correctly dressed. Inside the frescoes are very well preserved and you may be offered a glass of water from the sacred stream. The icon of Saint George is now kept in the monastery of Hozoviotissa[1].

Surrounding the monastery are beautiful gardens and the ruins of a water mill. Today water for the gardens comes from four nearby springs. Opposite the monastery on the summit of Skopoi are the remains of a square Venetian watchtower and nearby many important ancient relics have been found.

Valsamitis

Here was the sacred stream, the *aytatrna,* which flows into a marble basin, carefully kept clean with a sponge at hand for the purpose lest any extraneous matter should by chance get in. Thereupon he filled the tumbler and went to examine its contents in the sun's rays with a microscope that he might read my destiny. He then returned to the steps of the altar and solemnly delivered his oracle. The priests of St. George have numerous unwritten rules, which they hand down from one to the other, and which guide them in delivering their answers. Papa Anatolios told me many of them.

1. If the water is clear, with many white specks in it about the size of a small pearl, and if these sink but rise again, it signifies health and success but much controversy. I was a foreigner and a guest, so politely he prophesied this lot for me.

2. If there is a small white insect in the water, which rushes about hither and thither in the glass, there is no fear of storm or fire.

3. Black specks are bad, and indicate all sorts of misfortunes, according to their position in the water; if they float they are prospective. Some that appeared in my glass sank; these Papa Anatolios told me referred to difficulties of the past.

4. Hairs are often found therein; these indicate cares, ill-health, and loss of money. From these I was luckily exempt, but my unfortunate servant, who tried his luck after me, had lots in his glass. Poor man! He never recovered his peace of mind till dinner time, when the enlightened demarch laughed at his fears and told him some reassuring anecdotes.

5. When you ask a direct question concerning matrimony or otherwise the wily priest regulates his answers by these microscopic atoms which float in the glass. If the marble bowl is empty at Easter time the year will be a bad one; if full the contrary. This is easily accounted for by the rainfall. These and many other points Papa Anatolios told me, and I thanked him for letting me off so mercifully. To my surprise on offering him a remuneration for opening to me the oracle he flatly refused and seemed indignant.

Bent, James Theodore. 1885. *The Cyclades or Life among the Insular*

Walk Information

The bus from Chora to Kolofana passes by the monastery and can be asked to stop there. There are buses from Katapola at the end. There is a small car park at the monastery which saves the short walk down the access road. Water should be carried, especially in the summer. If sticking to the main walk described boots are not required. It is downhill all the way starting at the road at 258m and finishing at sea level.

---

[1] See Walk 6

[For the really intrepid[1]; from WP3 you can turn right and follow the wall of the monastery around until you are just below the building and then work your way down to the river bed. You can then follow this all the way down to WP7 and onto Katapola. It must be stressed that there is no path, it is a scramble. You will be fighting your way through dense undergrowth in places and faced with many deep drops and cliffs. In the spring you may even be wading through water and sliding down waterfalls. This is one of our hidden places. You will not even find a goatherd down there, only goats. If the 'Lady loves Milk Tray' this is the route for you, but you have been warned. Do not go alone, take another commando with you.]

Instructions

	From the main road (1) follow the access road down to *Agios Valsamitis* (2).
486	After visiting the monastery take the slope up to the right and proceed through the gate ahead. Continue along past the springs, watermill and gardens to the next gate along (3).
141	Continue straight along the path until the corner (4) [You may at this point bear left and follow the path seen on the map to go down to Katapola via Minoa[2]].
536	Just before the sign post to Minoa turn right at the cairn and the rocky mound towards Katapola. Pass through the gate in the fence and go straight ahead passing above the farm. Head for the castle-looking buildings on the small peak ahead with Katapola in view down and slightly to your left. Go straight ahead descending along the top of the ridge. Just before the perimeter walls of the 'castle' bear left down the slope passing to the left and just below the structure (5).
517	Weave left down the slope towards the stream bed below. Follow this path down to the bottom and proceed ahead with the wall of the reservoir to your left. Bear right to follow the wall along to the top of the reservoir (6) This is not actually a reservoir per se but a flood defence system for Katapola.
883	Turn sharp left to proceed to the dam (7).
180	Cross the dam and turn right at the end down the road to the gate and follow the road into Katapola coming out on the front by the war memorial (8).
1,000	

---

[1] See Title verso: author's disclaimer
[2] See Walk 10

GPS Waypoints

No.	Latitude and Longitude (Degrees and Minutes)	Elevation (m)
1	N36° 48.392 E025° 52.789	258
2	N36° 48.489 E025° 52.623	240
3	N36° 48.586 E025° 52.601	238
4	N36° 48.756 E025° 52.335	213
5	N36° 48.995 E025° 52.271	133
6	N36° 49.135 E025° 52.379	29
7	N36° 49.254 E025° 52.243	35
8	N36° 49.682 E025° 51.966	0

River bed below Valsamitis

Area of Ancient Arkesini (Kato Meria)

General Notes on the area

The area of Kato Meria (Lower Land) is relatively flat with little terracing required to farm the land and traditionally was the main farming area on the island. Although the soil is very fertile farming is made harder by low rainfall and in the past led to many people leaving the area. Thus Kato Meria has a very small ageing population living in the comparatively small villages of Vroutsi, Kamari, Kolofana and Arkesini. With no port and until the road was completed Kato Meria was somewhat inaccessible and was considered poorer and less developed than the rest of the island. It is believed that the first settlers on the island in the Neolithic period settled in this area. Near Kamari at Markiani are the remains of an extensive settlement dating to the early Cycladic period. This area in ancient times was controlled by the ancient city of Arkesini, which is located on a promontory near to Vroutsi and was established in the 10th - 8th century BC and occupied until the medieval era.

Olive picking

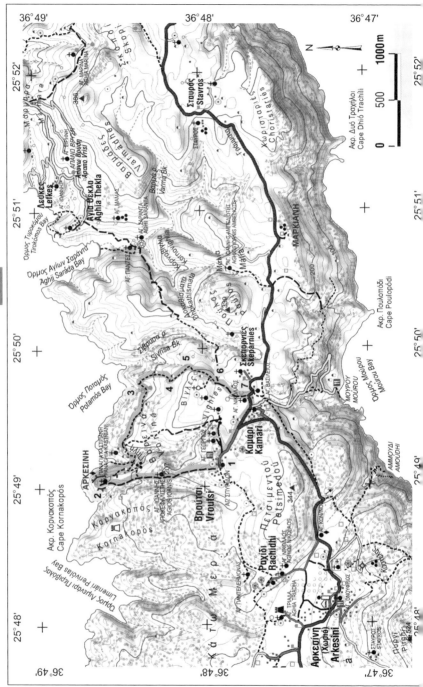

Walk 9 Ancient Arkesini

Walk 9 Ancient Arkesini (5.5 kms)

This is a delightful short walk without too much climbing on a good path which is slightly overgrown in places. It takes you to one of the three ancient cities on the island and along a beautiful coastal path. Passing springs and fertile areas, it is very colourful in the spring. There are many nice views across the sea to neighbouring islands. It is interesting historically and for the nature.

Places of Interest

Stavros

This Byzantine church, just before Kamari (see map), is built on an ancient site and lies on the border that separated the areas controlled by ancient Minoa and Arkesini. About a half kilometre away an ancient stone bearing the inscription 'oros' (boundary) has been found.

Ancient Arkesini

The ancient city of Arkesini was first established in the 10th to 8th centuries BC by settlers from Naxos and was inhabited until the middle ages when it was

---

The Police

Michalis a shopkeeper, barber and donkey saddle-maker extraordinaire, when much younger, was always very friendly with the police as he used to cut their hair. His mother also used to cook and clean at the police station so, as a family, they were very well informed as to what was happening there, both officially and privately. He recalls one policeman called Themis who never removed his hat except of course to have his hair cut. This wasn't a long job as he was almost completely bald, about which he had an enormous complex; thus the hat. Some village wag had told him that the best way to restore a head of hair was to shave your entire head regularly and in time it would all grow back. Taking this advice, hook, line and sinker he would regularly go to Michalis for a head shave. For his daily face shave at the barbers his hat would stay firmly in place but the head shave required almost surgical removal of 'the hat'. Michalis was of course sworn to secrecy and Themis provided his own razor, apparently for security reasons. Whilst this delicate operation was taking place the door had to be closed and Michalis was not to speak to anyone who called from outside or knocked on the door. Due to all of this Michalis was of course highly trusted by the police. It was for this reason that early one evening Themis turned up at his house and asked if there was somewhere he could hide. Michalis obliged and locked him in his kitchen assuming that someone was out to take revenge upon him for some incident involving his police duties. During the course of the evening it transpired that the Chief of Police had rostered Themis to do a night patrol and he was scared stiff. This was purely because he was afraid of the dark and in all his time in the police force had always managed to avoid said duty.

Out of the Rat Race into the Fire

abandoned due to the threat from pirates. There is evidence of extensive quarrying in the area in ancient times. During the early Cycladic period, walls, buildings and defensive towers were constructed and many relics, inscriptions, sculptures and pottery from this era have been found. There is also evidence that during the 3rd – 2nd centuries BC that there was regular contact with Rithymna in Crete. During the Geometric and Roman periods an ancient underground aqueduct was formed into an arched water cistern. Roman tombs have been found, along with an acropolis dedicated to Aphrodite and Athena, and a road that was lined with colonnades and inscribed steles. During the Venetian period extra fortifications were built. Today many of the ancient structures can still be seen.

Today the area is still used for some agriculture and grazing goats. The chapel of Panagia Kastriani is unfortunately locked as it reputedly contains some very special icons.

Walk Information

This is a very pleasant stroll and the path is good. Boots are not really required. It can however be a little overgrown in places. Some water should be carried, especially if it is hot. The bus from Chora stops in Vroutsi and can be stopped in Kamari. This route can be combined with walk 10 by turning left at WP6 towards the end. Starting and finishing at 265m the route descends to the base of the Kastri (96m) and then gently climbs and descends to the head of two coves the lowest point being 60m.

Instructions

Starting at the church (1) in Vroutsi[1] go up the slope and take the first right turning signposted to *Ancient Arkesini*. Follow the path all the way down to pass to the left of Agios Yannis. Continue on down and then up to the base of the Kastri (2).

1,430   After coming down from the ancient site go straight ahead and up through the gate just to the left of your arrival point. Following the path up the slope turn left at the threshing circle to follow the path down. Continue around the head of the cove turning left to climb up the other side. Follow the path along the coast, with a view of Chora in the distance, to the head of the next cove (3).

1,430   Cross the stream bed and go up the other side turning right at the top. Follow the path along for another 320m then turn right up over the wall and up onto the ridge ahead. Follow the stream bed to your right. At the top bear left along the terracing and through the gap in the wall at the top (4).

540   Go straight ahead through the undergrowth heading for the farm on the ridge above (5).

[1] See History

270	Go down the left hand side of the farm house and turn right to follow the path ahead up the terracing. At the top turn left above the water cistern and carry on along the path. Turn left at the end down to the main path (6) to Kamari[1].
470	Turn right onto this path and follow it to Kamari (7).
440	Turn right onto the main road back to Vroutsi.
930	

GPS Waypoints

No.	Latitude and Longitude (Degrees and Minutes)	Elevation (m)
1	N36° 47.893 E025° 49.132	265
2	N36° 48.569 E025° 49.039	96
3	N36° 48.335 E025° 49.713	75
4	N36° 48.186 E025° 49.825	152
5	N36° 48.083 E025° 49.922	179
6	N36° 47.901 E025° 49.743	214
7	N36° 47.724 E025° 49.660	230

Agios Yannis

---

[1] See Walk 10

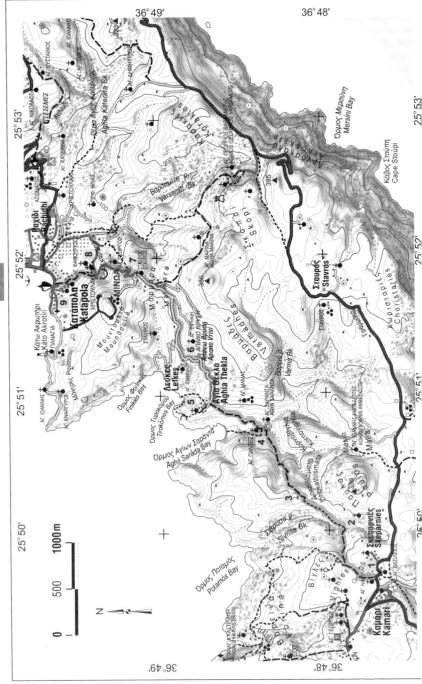

Walk 10 Kamari to Minoa

Walk 10 Kamari to Minoa   (6.7 kms)

Following the ancient road (still visible) from Ancient Arkesini to Minoa this route starts in Kamari and finishes in Katapola. You walk through an area where mankind first settled on Amorgos in Neolithic times. It is one of the most fertile areas of the island and as you approach Agii Saranda there are flowering oleanders along the river bed which runs into the bay. The spring from above the bay results in water flowing down here well into the summer. Just above Katapola is the ancient city of Minoa. From Minoa a new paved road has been built but after a short walk down this the route takes you onto an old donkey path with an attractive walk down into the narrow passages above the port.

Places of Interest

Kamari
The village of Kamari is built on the site of an ancient settlement and many artefacts from the Byzantine era have been found in the area. Next to the starting point of the walk is the triple church of Saint Nicholas in which rare Byzantine frescoes have been found under the more modern whitewash. In the chapel to the left the Byzantine frescoes of the Saints are in fairly good condition; however, non-Christian invaders gouged out their eyes during the days of piracy. From Kamari there is a road that leads to Mouros, which has a pebbly beach, deep clear blue water and caves. It is excellent for snorkelling. Just above the beach is a taverna and bar that are open in the high season.

Agii Saranda
The bay of Agii Saranda (Forty Saints) and the surrounding area were first inhabited in the Early Cycladic period. The Varmas gorge carries water down from the mountains, which finally drains into the bay usually well into summer when it eventually dries up. Many springs also provide plenty of water for most of the year. Up until recent times many small settlements in this area were still inhabited and the terraced land established in ancient times is still farmed. The double chapel just above the bay is built on the site of an ancient temple and many stones used in its construction date from the 5th century BC. Up until a few years ago within the screen of the chapel was a valuable Byzantine icon depicting the Forty Saints; it has been professionally restored and is now kept in the monastery of Hozoviotissa for security. It is currently on display next to the screen in the chapel.

Lefkes
The small village of Lefkes is where the Greek scholar Emmanuel Ionnides (1823-1906) was born. He spent many years studying Greek folklore and recorded the historical and cultural heritage of Amorgos. When he died he left behind a rare private collection of books comprising of over 1000 volumes. During his lifetime he also collected many artefacts found either by him or by locals; these now form the basis for the archaeological collection in Chora.

Minoa

The ancient city of Minoa was situated on Mondoulia above the port of Katapola and is where the most extensive modern excavations on the island have taken place. The archaeologist L. Ross first identified the site in 1837 followed by G. Deschamps who carried out the first excavations in 1888. Unfortunately no accurate records were kept but it appears that the excavations concentrated on the Hellenistic and Roman remains. In 1894 and 1981 the Archaeological Society at Athens performed the first systematic survey and small-scale excavations dating the first occupation of the summit and northeast slope to the Late Neolithic period. The southern slope was identified as having been first occupied in the Cycladic period with the nucleus of the lower city being established in the 10th century BC. Since 1981 the University of Ioannina under the supervision of Professor Lila Marangou has continued excavation of the site. The remains that can be seen today date from the Hellenistic and Roman periods with much evidence buried below or destroyed by long and continuous occupation.

Under the Hellenistic and Roman remains archaeologists have found a large pit hewn into the rock that was filled with an ash deposit. The ash contained animal bones, seashells, fish bones, metal objects, sea pebbles and potsherds dating from the 9th-7th centuries BC and probably come from either burnt sacrifices or ritual meals. Athenian pottery was also found bearing inscriptions stating 'Athenians settled on Amorgos under Naxian leadership'.

Located on the upper terraces the remains of a few buildings have been found along with a Hellenistic pottery workshop. Hewn into the rock are seven steps leading up to the cult area that were still in use in the 4th century BC when the marble main gate was built.

A grave enclosure dating to the 9th-8th centuries BC has been found, and the remains of twelve funerary pyres and an infant pot burial located. Grave offerings present include iron weaponry, bronze jewellery, clay spindle whorls, and libation pots indicating that the people buried here were either from the aristocracy or were founders of the city. The later building of a high stone wall around the cemetery and the fact that this area became the most eminent part of the city supports the theory that the people buried there were considered to have been very important.

The Acropolis was first established in the late 8th- early 7th century BC and at this time protective walls and bastions were built. The sanctuary has been partly excavated and filled in again for protection. A temple-like room with other rooms connected to it was revealed including one room containing a bench for votives and an altar. Finds include obsidian blades, fragments of pottery, animal bones, seashells and charcoal from fires. Many of these artefacts were found undisturbed in rock cavities and may have been placed there during the Prehistoric period indicating that the area was used as a religious site before the Acropolis was formally established. The deities worshipped here seem to have evolved over the centuries. Initially the people probably worshipped a chthonic or hero cult centred

Spring in the mountains

around a foundation myth connected to King Minos of Crete (hence the story of King Minos having a summer palace at Minoa). By the 7th- 6th centuries BC a cult dedicated to Dionisios had developed that was associated with fertility and growth. Increasing contact with Egypt resulted in the cult of Dionysis merging with Egyptian gods especially Serapis, Osiris and Isis. There is evidence that houses and roads also existed in this area until the site was abandoned in the 4th century BC.

During the 7th century BC settlers from Samos founded the more modern nucleus of the city. There is evidence of continuous occupation and contacts with Paros, Ionia, Samos and Athens. The building of the Theatre, Bouleutterion, Stoa of Agora and Temple dedicated to Dionysos Minotis were constructed in the Hellenistic period. The remains that can still be seen are parts of the marble gate, retaining terrace wall, Temple, Gymnasium, toilets, water cistern and drainage channel. The Temple is situated in the old cult area with the mosaic floor and headless statue thought to be of Apollo remaining. Nearby a pottery workshop has been found with clay reservoirs, a well, pottery kiln and supply channel. The Gymnasium was identified in 1984 and was built in the most important part of the city. In 1986 the toilets were found with the roof intact and the walls plastered and decorated with red, yellow, green and white slip. A drainage channel covered with stone slabs was also found at this time. In this area were also found five large pithos jars that would have been used to store olive oil.

The Roman period was a time when Amorgos became a place of political exile and consequently became more important. In the 2nd century AD a monumental cistern was built behind the Gymnasium and within its foundations an Early Cycladic idol has been found. The youngest coins found in the Minoa area date from the 3rd century AD and support the theory that the city was finally abandoned in the 4th century AD due to the increasing importance of the port of Katapola. The land was gradually modified and covered by farmers using the area for cultivation and grazing.

Today the archaeological site is fenced off to protect it, despite efforts a few years ago to make walkways for visitors. This project may be completed in the future. Usually in the summer months information boards are displayed describing the site in Greek and English. There is a marked path leading up the hill that offers a stunning view of Katapola.

Walk information

Starting in Kamari in Kato Meria this walk finishes in Katapola. The bus from Chora to Kolofana will stop on request in Kamari. There are buses from Katapola at the end of the walk. The path is very well paved all the way and just a good pair of shoes would suffice. It is a protected and maintained route so should not be overgrown. There are no places to buy water on the whole route. There are springs but the water quality can't be guaranteed. The walk starts at a taverna but it is not always open, there are no shops in Kamari. It is advisable to arrive at the start point with supplies for the walk. There are no short cuts but once you start on this delightful route you will want to continue anyway. Starting at 126m you drop down to sea level Agii Saranda (WP4) rising to 246m if you go to the top of Minoa and then dropping down to the port of Katapola.

Ripe Olives

Shopping

A little later that morning we went to see Agiris just to buy some bread and eggs, yet another shopping adventure. There were six other people in the shop waiting to be served, all visitors to the island. As we entered they were ignored as if they didn't exist. We were welcomed like long lost friends and 'Raki, Raki?' was shouted at us as if it was some sort of informal greeting rather than rocket fuel. This locally produced clear liquor is about nine hundred percent proof and certainly not to be taken internally. Agiris had just taken delivery of a very large keg of the stuff which can be bought loose if you bring along your own bottle. It is recommended to use one that has been made for ICI to transport sulphuric acid. His wife manages their other shop in the next village and Agiris is using this guaranteed freedom from discovery to hold parties in and outside his shop with this keg of Raki as a source of leglessness and blurred vision. As the controller of supplies and as the FD, MD and chairman of the operation all rolled into one, his wife without doubt would have well and truly killed him if she knew what was going on. What looked like a British Rail plastic beaker was produced and half filled with the liquor. The tourists looked on contemplating the commercial opportunities for opening a drying out clinic on the island as I set to with the rocket fuel, my Greek improving considerably with every mouthful. Whilst I was trying to keep on an even keel and focus on the cup Henri selected a loaf from the top of the breadbasket on the counter. It was unceremoniously whipped from her hand and Agiris disappeared head first into a huge sack behind the counter and reappeared proffering an identical loaf. He thrust his index finger deep into the centre of it to demonstrate the freshness of said item and the offending original was replaced in the basket for the next unsuspecting foreigner. Trays of eggs were prominent on the counter but when 'avga' were requested yet another disappearing act was called for as he delved deep into a large fridge at the back of the shop. 'These were laid this morning by my chickens and are the best on the island', we were told. The problem with most local produce is that some is not available on the open market, they are all part of the island wide barter system. No tally is kept as to who owes what to whom, you just give people what you can or help out when you can, the theory being that it all balances out in the end. Thus there was no charge for the eggs. We left the shop with slightly blurred vision, half a dozen eggs and one loaf resembling an enormous doughnut, all for the price of the bread.

Out of the Rat Race into the Fire

Instructions

As you enter *Kamari* there is a taverna (1) set up off the road to the right. The start of this walk is down the path just next to it. Follow the path straight down to the bridge over the stream (2).

902   Follow the path as it turns slightly to the left and climbs the slope ahead to a farm house (3).

628   Turn right to go past the farm house on your left and follow the path down straight ahead. To get past the farm you may have to work your way through one or two 'Greek gates', please close them after you. Follow the path as it zigzags down the slope to *Agii Saranda* (4).

1,210   Cross the stream bed at the bottom and continue up the slope straight ahead until you come to a few houses at Thekla (5).

710 Bear right to continue on the wide dirt track as it curves around the top of Tirokomos (cheese maker) bay to *Lefkes* (6).

780 From Lefkes keep following the road along around Finikes bay to the turning for *Minoa* (7).

1,300 At this point turn left up the slope to visit this ancient and fascinating excavated site. From WP7 continue down on the concrete road towards Katapola[1]. After weaving down the road you come to a 180° right hand bend under a scary-looking rock over-hang. Just after this corner before the little church is a mule track down to the left (8).

730 Follow this track down to the port of Katapola turning left around the church and right at the bottom of the steps.

460

GPS Waypoints

No.	Latitude and Longitude (Degrees and Minutes)	Elevation (m)
1	N36° 47.727 E025° 49.645	217
2	N36° 47.901 E025° 49.999	126
3	N36° 48.149 E025° 50.235	188
4	N36° 48.383 E025° 50.745	0
5	N36° 48.700 E025° 50.932	94
6	N36° 48.842 E025° 51.271	97
7	N36° 49.122 E025° 51.897	170
8	N36° 49.370 E025° 51.899	70
9	N36° 49.600 E025° 51.832	0

Spring on Amorgos

---

[1] See Walk 7

Winter in the UK

For the first two years of living on Amorgos we went back to the UK for the winter. It takes some time to readjust to life away from the island. Apparently you need to carry money with you, Waitrose will not let you pay next week. The smaller shops and bars don't like you helping yourself off the shelves and just walking out. You have to show a tax disc on your vehicle and carry papers for the car. You can't fall out of a bar into your Land Rover and then expect the policeman waiting for you to join you for another drink. You can't merely park in the middle of the road and expect people to just wait for you to return without offering derogatory remarks about your parentage. You don't stop every time you see another car coming the other way and expect him to stop for a chat. You can't just leave your shopping in the street whilst you pop in to have lunch with friends without people thinking it is a charitable handout. You cannot leave your wallet on a wall and expect it to be still there two days later when you return. You are considered a little odd if you greet everyone you pass in Oxford street with a cheery hello. You never get home to find piles of donated groceries and the odd fish or lump of lamb on your doorstep. The manager of Waitrose doesn't force you to drink rocket fuel at nine o'clock in the morning, although this may be a blessing.

You can however turn on a tap and get water out of it and expect electricity and telephones to be connected to your house. You can drive right up to your home and don't need to hire a donkey to deliver heavy goods. You don't expect the doctor to discuss your ailments and potential remedies with all and sundry at your local pub. You can get to a dentist, optician, or a vet without spending two days on a boat in a force eight gale. You can have television programmes beamed right into your sitting room so that you can fester in front of some Australian soap opera every evening. You can have the post delivered to your door daily and find piles of bills on the doormat to worry about and give you high blood pressure. You can also get stuck in traffic jams and experience or practice road rage and stress. You can sit at a comfortable desk and work a forty-hour week; trapped in an office in a noisy polluted city. You can eat food that, if you are lucky, only contains about twenty different chemicals. Best of all you can work in the city all your life and expect a pension when you retire wondering why the actuary has been so generous with the returns. There is life and then there is 'Life'. For us there is only one course to follow, and that is a donkey track leading: 'Out of the Rat Race Back into the Fire'. That was our last winter in the UK.

Out of the Rat Race into the Fire

Walk Options

Included in this guide are some 'optional extras' not described in detail. Some walks cross or overlap so there is the opportunity of combining walks for a longer day out. The maps enclosed are all to the same scale (1:40,000) and from accurate Topos by Anavasi. Many more paths are available and walks can be extended by using these routes. We have purposely included large full page areas of map that are not needed for each route expressly for this purpose. All maps you will need for walks described are enclosed. However, the more intrepid may wish to purchase the topo of the whole island which is available from Anavasi[1], or can be purchased locally.

On a long thin island it is difficult to plan circular walks so some routes are 'one way' or 'back the same way'. However, experience dictates that taking the same path in the opposite direction can often seem like a completely different walk with views not noticed on the way out. The authors are well aware of the problems with public transport on the island especially in low season. 'One way' walks have been planned to start where there may not necessarily be a bus stop but the driver will drop you off. In this case be explicit and even point to the place on the map in the book for him. The conclusion of these walks have been planned to place you in a good position for a more frequent bus service. Some clients of Special Interest Holidays have teamed up with another couple to hire a car for one way walks and for each team to walk the route in opposite directions swapping over the keys half way. You do however have to be very trusting with this arrangement in case the other couple give up, turn back and fall into a taverna for the day!

Coffee outside Nikos' Taverna, Langada

[1] See Appendix

Theologos

Appendix

Departing Ormos on the ship

Getting to Amorgos and around the Island

Ships
There is a regular service all year around from the port of Piraeus to Amorgos. These ships usually operate six times a week. There are two ports on the island; Katapola and Aegiali. The service alternates between the two and takes about eight hours. The ships are large, modern and comfortable with excellent en-suite cabins. These ships usually pass through Paros and Naxos on their way so provide a good connection with these two islands. In the summer this service is supplemented with extra ships including high speed vessels. Additionally, in the summer there are usually connections to Santorini and other nearby islands. Schedules constantly change and should be monitored carefully either by phoning a shipping agent or checking on the internet (see useful sites). In high season or on national holidays it is advisable to book your tickets[1] well in advance.

Flights
There is no airport on Amorgos but there is a heliport for medical evacuation and helicopter charters. The nearest and most convenient airport is Naxos. A ship from there can take as little as two hours. There are also airports on Santorini and Astypalia.

Buses
There is a regular bus service on the island. It varies in frequency depending on the time of year. It can also change with very little notice. Bus time tables are posted at various places. The most reliable ones are at the bus stops or in the window of the bus to check your return.

Taxis
There are a few taxis on the island. There is no taxi rank and you can't just flag one down, they have to be booked. There are various notices around the island with telephone numbers including at most bus stops. A taverna or hotel owner will always be able to supply you with a telephone number or order you one. The best number to get is for the driver's mobile phone. Do not expect to get a taxi instantly - it may take hours, and it is always best to book in advance. Do not expect to get a taxi in the middle of the night (unless you book) and if you need one to meet you at the port also book in advance as they are all busy when the ship arrives or departs. Your hotel owner should be able to help you with a taxi for your arrival. Many of the hotels have buses to meet clients upon arrival but ensure they know which ship you are on. It is always a good idea to phone to remind them when you are actually on the ship.

Hire vehicles
There are a number of companies who hire out cars, motorbikes and quad bikes. One or two of them have a small minibus. They are strictly regulated and you will need all your papers with you to hire. Their prices are all similar but it is worth

---

[1] See Useful Web Sites

Missing the Ship

Tim and David, two management consultants, were helping us to set up a management-training programme on the island; we met up in Naxos. We planned to catch the 11.30 Jorgos Express on to Amorgos with them. We said that we would go ahead to the quay and left them sorting out their hotel bills, we had plenty of time. Walking down the quay I could see one large ferry already in but it wasn't until we got much closer that I could see that it was the Jorgos Express. The ferries do sometimes hold at Naxos for a few hours so I wasn't over concerned about this early arrival but I asked Henri to go over and check it was still planning to go on time. She wandered over and with great difficulty extracted the information from the port police that it had changed its departure time at 21.00 the previous night from 11.30 to 11.00. It was now 10.50 and Tim and David were nowhere to be seen. I dropped my briefcase and jacket and ran the full length of the quay which is a good two hundred yards. I found my two colleagues settling down to a coffee on the front. 'Leaving, boat, our, run, now' I shouted, in a millisecond they had rearranged these words into a meaningful sentence; this is why they are management consultants. They made order out of chaos and then resorted to chaos themselves as they threw aside their chairs and threw money in approximately the right direction of the waiter. Their suitcases were in a baggage storage area in the information centre next door. Forgoing the formalities of handing over tickets and gently extracting the bags under supervision I shouted to Tim to identify his bags. He pointed at his luggage, a matching set of two black bags. He was carrying a large briefcase so I just grabbed them for him and ran. David grabbed his bag and brought up the rear. Give them both their due, the most exercise they normally get is climbing in and out of cars and pushing a trolley around Waitrose, but they did run. This would have all been hunky dory if that was all that was required but Tim also needed to communicate; it required spare lung capacity which he just didn't have available at that moment in time. He took advantage of a one second stop to avoid us being run over, 'mine, bags, those, isn't, one, of' he panted. Again all being in the same game, I worked this out in an instant and threw the offending item back into the office. We ran the full length of the quay. Four minutes to spare, fifty yards to go and the ramp started to rise. The port policeman shouted for them to stop, they ignored him. We stopped at the now rising ramp as they cast off one of the two hawsers, I shouted up at the officer controlling the operation from the stern. his reaction was to just raise his hands, cast off the second hawser and pull away four minutes early on the revised departure time. We caught a flying dolphin that was fortunately running later that afternoon with Tim and David both on stretchers.

Out of the Rat Race into the Fire

shopping around. The prices vary according to the season. You will get a discount for the longer you hire. Most companies are not concerned about the amount of fuel left when you return the vehicle. To this end be aware that you may be given a vehicle which has hardly any fuel remaining and indeed this is usually the case. There are many motorbike accidents on the island every year. There are countless hairpin bends and when it is windy it is easy to go round a corner into a gust of wind and be blown off. For four people it is almost the same price to hire a car as two bikes. This is well worth thinking about and may save you having an accident, unless of course you want a free helicopter ride to hospital!

National Holidays and Amorgos Festivals

Greek National Holidays and Local Festivals.

National Holidays

January 1st	New Year's Day
January 6th	Epiphany
1st Monday of Lent	Clean Monday
March 25th	Oxi Day (Anniversary celebrating start of War of Independence 1821)
Greek Orthodox Easter	(Good Friday to Easter Monday inclusive)
May 1st	May Day
Late May	Spring Holiday
August 15th	Panagia
August 28th	Oxi Day (Anniversary of Greece entering World War Two 1940)
December 25th/26th	Christmas

Local Festivals

Major Festivals on Amorgos

January 6th	Blessing of the sea- Ports of Aegiali and Katapola
Last Sunday before the start of Lent - Kapitanios- Langada	
March 25th	Annuciation- Parades in Chora, Langada and Katapola
May 8th	Monastery of Theologos
Sixth Thursday after Easter - Analipsis, Potamos	
July 1st	Agii Anargiri, Tholaria
July 26th	Agia Paraskevi, Paradisia
August 6th	Christos- Chora
August 15th	Panagia, Langada
September 14th	Stavros- Aegiali and near Kamari
September 26th	Monastery of Theologos
November 21st	Monastery of Hozoviotissa

Etiquette

Amorgos is a very traditional and old-fashioned community. The people are exceptionally friendly and will not be upset when a visitor to their island doesn't understand their customs and way of life. However, visitors should know at least a few points of etiquette in order to reciprocate the warm welcome they receive.

The most important points involve the Greek Orthodox Church. If you are not Greek Orthodox it is not advisable to enter any large village church without being invited, indeed most of these are locked to prevent this happening. Some churches and monasteries however do welcome visitors. In churches and monasteries Gentlemen should wear trousers and Ladies should wear skirts that extend at least to the knee. For the ladies a wraparound shift over the top of shorts or trousers is most acceptable. Everyone should have their shoulders covered and ladies are not allowed behind the altar screen.

Walkers are particularly welcome on Amorgos because they learn more about the island and its people than most visitors. To this end you will find the local people particularly generous towards you. They will give you flowers, bunches of grapes, cheese, figs, pomegranates, etc. as you pass. It will slightly offend them if you refuse. In these cases it is worth noting that donkeys will eat almost anything! And, there are plenty of donkeys.

There are some fantastic photo opportunities on the island. One small point worth noting though is that generally the older ladies do not like having their photograph taken; there is no harm in asking though. In complete opposition to this the older generation of men usually love it and will pose for you. If it comes out well send a copy back to them, you'll be a friend for life.

Stroumbos

Rare and Protected Species of Flora on Amorgos

From: 'Natura 2000', EU Guidelines: Amorgos, 12.6.96

Akkium luteoloum
Anthemis scopulorum
Anthyllis aegaea
Asperula abbreviate
Asperula tournefortii
Aurunia saxatilis ssp. Saxatilis
Campanula heterophylla
Campanula laciniata
Centaurea oliverana
Centaurea raphanina mixta   Christ's thorn
Dianthus fruticosus
Eryngium Amorginum
Erysimum senoneri ssp. Amorginum
Fibigia lunarioides
Galium amorginum

Helichrysum Amorginum   Stathouri
Nepeta melissiofolia
Origanum tournefortii   Kefalohorto
Salsola aegaea
Scorzonera eximia
Sesseli gummiferum ssp.   Crithmifolium
Symphytum davisii   Comfrey
Anacamptis pyramidalis   Pyramidal orchid
Helichrysum orientale
Lactuca acanthitolia
Senecio bicolour
Campanula Amorgina rech.   Amorgean bell
Calendula arvensis   The old woman's spindle
Teucrium flavum   Dontohorti

Ornithology

Amorgos birds – a provisional list

compiled by
Dr Anthony Cheke, 139 Hurst St, Oxford OX4 1HE
anthony.cheke@innerbookshop.com

This list has been compiled from observations by Anthony & Ruth Cheke and Derek & Liz Hardy in September 2007, combined with the only previous records, given by Magioris (1994), indicated by '[M]' in the list below – he did not give any indication of status, just a list of birds reported. The list below follows Mullarney & others (1999, Collins Bird Guide) except where noted. The 2007 observations were concentrated mainly in the Aegiali area. 'Aegiali' is used for the district of that name, Ormos for the port.

NB: Amorgos has very depauperate habitat diversity with low (c350mm/yr) rainfall, currently lacking both forest and wetland, hence the absence of many species that would otherwise be expected. Much of the island is sparse dry *phrygana* (garrigue) dominated by the shrubby spurge *Euphorbia dendroides*. The drier areas are characterised by Lentisc *Pistacia lentiscus* and *Calicotome* spp., whereas in (relatively) wetter areas (e.g. the north slope of the Kroukelos range) there is denser *phrygana* dominated by Spanish broom *Spartium juncium* and Prickly or Holly Oak *Quercus coccifera*, developing in places into a maquis dominated by the latter.

The following list is presented in the format:
Name; Latin Name - Presumed Status - Actual Observations - Seen By

Levantine Shearwater[1]*Puffinus yelkouan* - may breed on offshore islets - not seen on Amorgos but seen from ferry to Dounoussa & Naxos; [M]-D&LH

Cory's Shearwater *Calonectris diomedea* - may breed on offshore islets - not seen on Amorgos but several seen from ferry off Naxos, 25/9; [M]-A&RC

Shag *Phalacrocorax aristotelis* - may breed on cliffs/small islets - 3 in Ormos bay 12/9; 1 there 25/9-A&RC

Mallard *Anas platyrhynchos* - ? - [M]-

Booted Eagle *Hieraetus pennatus* -? passage migrant - one only - D&LH

Bonelli's Eagle *H.fasciatus* - scarce presumed resident - 2 adults 15/9, 1 immature 23/9; all around Langada - A&RC

(Common) Buzzard *Buteo buteo* - common resident - seen daily around Aegiali - A&RC; D&LH

Honey Buzzard *Pernis apivorus* - ? passage migrant - 3 over Langada 16/9 - A&RC

Sparrowhawk *Accipiter nisus* - ? - [M] -

(Common) Kestrel *Falco tinnunculus* - common resident - seen daily around Aegiali - A&RC; D&LH

Lesser Kestrel *F.naumanni* - ? passage migrant - on cliffs above Langada, on several occasions - A&RC; D&LH

Eleonora's Falcon *F.eleonorae* - common summer visitor - seen daily around Aegiali; also on islets off Choviotissa; [M] - A&RC; D&LH

Peregrine *F.peregrinus* - probably resident - seen on several occasions around Aegiali - A&RC; D&LH

Chukar[2] *Alectoris chukar* - sparse resident - 2 adults & 3 juvenile seen crossing road near Langada, also on rock face above village & heard elsewhere on Kroukelos - A&RC; D&LH

Yellow-legged Gull[3]*Larus (cachinnans) micahellis* - presumed resident & breeder on offshore islets - seen daily in very small numbers in Ormos bay; [M] - A&RC; D&LH

Rock Dove *Columba livia* -resident - on cliffs & occasional small groups in fields [there are also free-flying domestic pigeons, mostly white]; [M] - A&RC

Collared Dove *Streptopelia decaocto* - common resident - only seen in villages & cultivation - A&RC; D&LH

Turtle Dove *S.turtur* - ? passage migrant - singles seen 15 & 17/9 near Langada, very shy - A&RC

Scops Owl *Otus scops* - presumed resident - heard at night in Langada in treed area around lower car park & cemetery - D&LH

Barn Owl *Tyto alba* - presumed resident - reported to D&LH by Nikos Vassalos - D&LH

Alpine Swift *Apus melba* - passage migrant, may breed ? -[would have left by mid-September] [M]-

Hoopoe *Upupa epops* - ? passage migrant - singles seen 17/9 at Ormos & in olive groves behind - A&RC

(European) Bee-eater *Merops apiaster* - passage migrant - groups of up to 30 on several days - A&RC; D&LH

(European) Roller *Coracias garrulous* - passage migrant - 1 in valley leading to Meghali Vichada bay (beyond Epanochoriani), 16/9; [M] -A&RC

Crested Lark *Galerida cristata* - common resident - commonest in cultivation, but also on dry hillsides - A&RC; D&LH

Short-toed Lark *Calandrella brachydactyla* - possibly resident - single birds on a few occasions, rarely confirmed to species - A&RC; D&LH

Crag Martin *Ptyonoprogne rupesris* - ? [may breed] - [M] -

(Barn) Swallow *Hirundo rustica* - passage migrant - 2 on 14/9 above Langada, & a flock of c20 a few days later; extraordinarily scarce, given how common swallows usually are on autumn passage everywhere! - A&RC

House Martin *Delichon urbica* - passage migrant; could breed on cliffs ? - 1 on 14/9 & a few some days later; same comment applies - A&RC; D&LH

Meadow/Tree Pipit *Anthus pratensis/trivialis* - passage migrant - seen regularly in Ormos garden plots behind beach, but species uncertain, either or both could occur - A&RC; D&LH

Pied ['White'] Wagtail *Motacilla alba* - passage migrant - 2 feeding round animals at Vassalos feedlot, 22/9; [M] - A&RC

Yellow Wagtail *M.flava* - passage migrant-widespread in small groups, usually associated with animals; [M] - A&RC

(Common) Redstart *Phoenicurus phoenicurus* - passage migrant - frequent in areas with trees - A&RC; D&LH

(Northern) Wheatear *Oenanthe oenanthe* - passage migrant; may breed ? - occasional in open habitat; [M] - A&RC; D&LH

Black-eared Wheatear *O.hispanica* - passage migrant; may breed ? -1 in valley inland of Fokiotripa (path to Tholaria), 18/9 + another later - A&RC; D&LH

Whinchat *Saxicola rubetra* - passage migrant, may breed-widespread but scattered; most common in cultivation behind Ormos - A&RC; D&LH

Stonechat *S.torquata* - probably resident - widespread in small numbers - A&RC; D&LH

Blue Rock Thrush *Monticola solitaries* - common resident - widespread but patchy on cliffs & rocky areas, visiting villages; [M] - A&RC; D&LH

Blackbird *Turdus merula* - ? scarce resident - [M]-

Garden Warbler *Sylvia borin* - passage migrant - 1 on several occasions in fruiting terebinth tree, Langada - A&RC

Blackcap *S.atricapilla* - common passage migrant - frequent in areas with broad-leaved trees, though avoids olives - A&RC; D&LH

Orphean Warbler *S.hortensis* - passage migrant; may breed ? - scarce but widespread in areas with trees, especially fruiting terebinth - A&RC; D&LH

Sardinian Warbler *S.melanocephala* - abundant resident - high densities wherever there is shrubbery - A&RC; D&LH

Whitethroat *S.communis* - passage migrant - 1 in fruiting terebinth, in valley inland of Fokiotripa (path to Tholaria), 18/9 + one or 2 others - A&RC

Sedge Warbler *Acrocephalus schoenobaenus* - passage migrant - 1 by fruiting terebinth, Langada, 24/9 (& a possible near Tholaria, 23/9) - A&RC

Olivaceous Warbler *Hippolais pallid* - passage migrant - 1 only, Langada - D&LH

Willow Warbler *Phylloscopus trochilus* - abundant passage migrant-rivalling Sardinian Warbler in abundance in September! - A&RC; D&LH

Chiffchaff *P.collybita* - passage migrant - only a few confirmed; much scarcer than Willow Warbler - A&RC; D&LH

Wood Warbler *P.sibilatrix* - passage migrant - one only - D&LH

Spotted Flycatcher *Muscicapa striata* - passage migrant, may breed-unexpectedly common wherever there were trees; [M] - A&RC; D&LH

Red-breasted Flycatcher *Ficedula parva* - passage migrant - seen regularly around the fruiting terebinth in Langada, also 1 at Theologos 22/9 - A&RC; D&LH

Pied-type flycatcher *Ficedula* sp. - passage migrant - male not identified to species, in valley inland of Fokiotripa (path to Tholaria), 17/9; 3 possible similar species[4] - A&RC

Red-backed Shrike *Lanius collurio* - passage migrant, may breed - frequent in areas with trees - A&RC; D&LH

Magpie *Pica pica* - ? - [M] -

Jackdaw *Corvus monedula* - ? - [M] -

Hooded Crow *C.(corone) cornix* -?, may breed -unexpectedly not seen by A&RC or D&LH; [M] -

Raven *Corvus corax* - common resident - the only corvid seen on the island ! [M] - A&RC; D&LH

Golden Oriole *Oriolus oriolus* - passage migrant - immature at 'Ancient Aegiali' (by Tholaria), 17/9 [& another seen early September by a client of P&H.D-R] - A&RC

House Sparrow *Passer domesticus* - common resident - in villages, cultivation & where donkeys are fed in remoter areas; [M] - A&RC; D&LH

Chaffinch *Fringilla coelebs* - ? resident - only record was a pair seen in prickly oaks near Theologos where there was access to water - A&RC

Linnet *Carduelis cannabina* - common resident - in small flocks in open areas - A&RC; D&LH

Goldfinch *C.carduelis* - resident - only seen in cultivation behind Langada; [M] - A&RC

Corn Bunting *Emberiza calandra* - ? scarce resident (grainfields) - [M] -

Birds likely to occur but not seen in September:
Mediterranean, Black-headed & Audouin's Gulls, swifts (? 3 species), Lesser Whitethroat, Icterine Warbler, Olive-tree Warbler, Serin (& no doubt other migrants)

References:

Magioris, Stavros N. 1994. The avifauna of the Cyclades (Aegean Sea). *Hellenic Zoological Archives* 2 (June 1994), 16pp.
Mullarney, Killian & others. 1999. *Collins bird guide / Birds of Europe*. London: Collins & Princeton NJ: Princeton University Press. 400pp.
Snow, David W. & Perrins, Christopher M. eds. 1998. *The birds of the western Palearctic. Concise edition.* Oxford: Oxford University Press. 2 vols.

---

[1] The old broadly defined Manx Shearwater is nowadays split into two (Mullarney & others 1999) or three (Perrins & Snow 1998) – the former *Puffinus puffinus yelkouan*, becoming *P.yelkouan*, Levantine or Yelkouan Shearwater.

[2] Although these we not positively identified to rule out Rock Partridge *A.graeca*, the only species known from the Cyclades in the Chukar [M].

[3] The Mediterranean (*micahellis*) and Black Sea/Caspian (*cachinnans*) races are often considered separate species; both were formerly considered races of the Herring gull *L.argentatus*.

[4] Pied, Collared and Semi-collared flycatchers (*Ficedula hypoleuca, F.albicollaris & F.semitorquata*) are very similar and any or all might be seen on passage – all three have been recorded on Paros, 2 on Naxos [M].

Eco-Tourism[1]

The authors' company Special Interest Holidays is dedicated to eco-tourism. They have been working on Amorgos and with other Greek islands to promote this concept since 1994.

Amorgos is about as unspoilt as any Greek island can be from undesirable development. This does not mean we can become complacent. Together with AITO, Elliniki Atairia, The Eco Club, Responsible Travel and the EU they are working to maintain the beauty and the traditional ethos of the island.

Of course there should be progress. However this has to be planned with eco-tourism in mind. There are places in the world where large tourist developments can take place without destroying the natural beauty of a destination and damaging the environment. These should not take place in unspoilt areas where visitors come to enjoy the nature and the tranquillity of a remote Greek island. Many destinations have already suffered from the bulldozer and millions of tons of concrete. Here on Amorgos we are not complacent. The beautiful area of Agios Pavlos, an ancient farming and fishing community, is currently threatened by developers with Euro signs in their eyes instead of the views of the mountains, the wildlife and the quiet rural scenes. Plans on drawing boards, such as the artist's impression in the picture below right, have to be opposed.

Short of a nuclear explosion there can be nothing more damaging to remote locations such as the Greek islands than sudden unplanned tourism development. The consequences to the physical environment may well destroy the very resource that attracted the tourist's attention in the first place. The rivers and coastlines become contaminated. The sea breeze carrying the aroma of herbs and flowers becomes polluted with exhaust emissions and aircraft fumes. The sounds of donkeys braying and the waves breaking on the beach are drowned out by beach discos and concrete mixers. Bright street lights block out the deep blue star sparkling Mediterranean night sky. There is congestion at the ports and in the villages that look more like London a week before Christmas, rather than a remote

---

[1] See appendix: Bibliography

Greek island. Road and hotel building causes soil erosion, damages vegetation and wildlife and destroys natural and ancient man-made features.

Income from tourism should not be ploughed back into further building it should be used to conserve and renovate existing resources. Here on Amorgos ruined old stables have been renovated and turned into holiday accommodation, ancient sites are being preserved and footpaths are maintained for visiting walkers and the local people alike. Conservation and the preservation of natural areas have emerged as important spill over benefits of tourism.

Eco-tourism is primarily the responsibility of the host community and country. However responsible travel is primarily down to the visitor and their tour operator. When planning a trip many aspects should be considered. Is it possible to fly just one sector instead of two to reduce carbon emissions? Read up on local cultures and how they are affected by tourism. Find out if there are local conservation projects at your destination that you could visit. If your holiday includes guides ensure that they are locally based. You will learn more and it is income for the community.

Eco-tourism and responsible travel is down to all stakeholders. Planners should consider the consequences of their proposals. Local authorities should think about the cost to the community when considering planning applications. When visitors go to an area for the nature and walking, more development is only going to reduce the community income not increase it. Travellers should research their proposed destination at the planning stage and consider the impact of their visit. This doesn't have to be negative there are many positive aspects to tourism.

Eco-tourism and responsible travel is the duty, of anyone who travels or is involved in the business. The jungles and rain forests are being destroyed and small Greek islands are being overdeveloped to the point of destruction. We can build bio-domes and reconstruct jungles and forests, although that is not the solution, but we can't reconstruct a Greek island or more importantly its ethos and family community.

The protection of the very resources that visitors come to enjoy enhances and perpetuates tourism by maintaining its very foundation.

Walk times and Conversions

It has been intentional not to suggest times for walks in this guide. The authors' experience with clients has identified that this can vary enormously. It depends on many factors which should be taken into account: fitness levels, the condition of paths, footwear, the temperature and the number in a group.

The internationally recognised rule of thumb for walk time calculations was devised by William W Naismith, a Scottish Mountaineer, in 1892:

1 hr for 5 kms/3 miles + ½ hr per 300m /1,000 ft climbed

This of course doesn't include stopping to admire the scenery, take photographs, to catch your breath or pop behind a tree! In reality these times should be considered as a minimum time to complete the route.

All distances and elevations in this guide are given in kilometres and metres.

Kms	Miles	Metres	Feet
0.5	0.31	50	164
1.0	0.62	100	328
2.0	1.25	200	656
3.0	1.86	300	984
4.0	2.49	400	1,312
5.0	3.11	500	1,640
6.0	3.73	600	1,968
7.0	4.35	700	2,296
8.0	4.97	800	2,624
9.0	5.59	900	2,952
10.0	6.21	1,000	3,280

Useful Web Sites

All about Amorgos including photo gallery, maps, walking information, holiday bookings, FAQs. Links for: weather, shipping schedules, ship booking, Greek phrases, currency conversion: www.walkingingreece.com

Local Botany: www.flowersofcrete.info

Birds of Greece: www.birdlist.org/greece

Amorgos Topo Maps: www.anavasi.gr

Alternative Eco-Tourism Holiday: www.safariholidaysbotswana.com

Bibliography

Alexiadou, Vefa. 1989. *Greek Cuisine*. Athens: Vefa Alexiadou.

Anastassiou, Tassos. 1996. *Amorgos. History. Sightseeing.* Hermoupolis: Archipelagos Cultural Corporation.

Anastassiou, Tassos. 2001. *A Travelogue of Amorgos.* Hermoupolis: Archipelagos Cultural Corporation.

Bent, James Theodore. 1885. *The Cyclades or Life among the Insular Greeks.* Chicago: Argonaut Inc. Chapter XIX. Amorgos pp 161- 171.

Burnie, David. 1995. *Wild Flowers of the Mediterranean.* London: Dorling Kindersley Limited.

Delahunt-Rimmer, P.R. 2006. *Eco-Tourism – Managing the Change.*

Deutsch, Mittheilungen des. 1876. *On the Greek Islands.* Archaol; Instituts. Pages 328- 332.

Facaros, Dana. 1994.*Greece: The Cyclades.* London: Cadogan Books plc.

Freeman, Charles. 1996. *Egypt, Greece and Rome.* Oxford. Oxford University Press.

Jonsson, Lars. 1992. *Birds of Europe.* London: Christopher Helm (Publishers) Ltd.

Mackenzie, Molly. 1989. *Amorgos. A Brief History and what to see.* Athens: Ioannis E. Despotidis.

Mackenzie, Molly. 2006. *Amorgos. The Story of a Greek Island.* Tbilisi: LINK.

Marangou, Lila. 2002. *Excavating Classical Culture. Recent archaeological discoveries in Greece.* Athens: BAR International Series 1031. Minoa on Amorgos pp 295- 316.

Marangou, Lila. 2000. *Archaelogical Collection of Amorgos : I Marble Sculptures.* Athens. Lila Marangou.

March, Jenny. 1998. *Dictionary of Classical Mythology.* London. Cassell

Mathieson, A. and Wall, G. 1982. *Tourism: Economic, physical and social impacts.* London and New York: Longman

Matsouka, Penelope. 2009. *Amorgos Map (2009 edition)* Athens: Anavasi.

Matthews, Carola. 1971. *At the top of the Mule Track.* London. Macmillan.

Witt, S.F. Brooke, M.Z. and Buckley, P.J. 1991. *The Management of International Tourism.* London and New York: Routledge

INDEX

NOTES

NOTES

NOTES